Traeger Grill & Smoker Cookbook

1000 Days of Delicious Recipes with Images, Tips, and Techniques for Perfecting Your BBQ Game!

By DR Esther

TABLE OF CONTENTS

INTRODUCTION

Welcome to the "Traeger Grill & Smoker Cookbook: 1000 Days Delicious Recipes, Tips, and Techniques for Perfecting Your BBQ Game!" This comprehensive guide is designed to help you become a BBQ master, no matter your experience level. With 1000 mouthwatering recipes, expert tips, and innovative techniques tailored specifically for your Traeger grill and smoker, this cookbook is your ultimate resource for elevating your grilling skills and impressing your friends and family with irresistible barbecue creations.

Whether you're a seasoned pitmaster or just starting your BBQ adventure, this cookbook has something for everyone. Each recipe is carefully crafted, with detailed instructions and ingredient lists, to help you achieve BBQ perfection. From succulent smoked meats to tempting sides and decadent desserts, you'll find everything you need to create delicious and memorable meals that will have your guests returning for more.

But that's not all - this cookbook is also packed with expert tips and techniques to help you take your grilling to the next level. Whether you're looking to perfect your smoking technique or learn how to make the perfect BBQ sauce, this guide has you covered. With step-by-step instructions and helpful photos, you can master even the most challenging recipes and techniques.

So, get ready to fire up the grill, ignite your passion for cooking outdoors, and embark on an unforgettable culinary odyssey with the "Traeger Grill & Smoker Cookbook" as your trusted companion. With this comprehensive guide, you'll be well on your way to becoming the ultimate BBQ master in no time.

EXPERT TIPS AND TECHNIQUES TO HELP YOU MASTER THE ART OF SMOKING AND GRILLING.

Mastering the art of smoking and grilling requires a combination of technique, knowledge, and practice. Here are some expert tips and techniques that you might find in the "Traeger Grill & Smoker Cookbook":

Choosing the Right Wood: Different types of wood impart distinct flavours to your food. Experiment with woods like hickory, mesquite, apple, cherry, or oak to find the best flavours that complement your ingredients.

Preheating: Preheat your grill or smoker to the desired temperature before adding your food. This ensures even cooking and helps prevent sticking.

Indirect Heat: Your grill should have both direct and indirect heat zones. Direct heat is great for searing, while indirect heat is ideal for slow smoking. Learn to manage these zones for different cooking techniques.

Temperature Control: Invest in a quality thermometer to accurately monitor the temperature of your grill and your food. Maintaining consistent temperatures is crucial for achieving perfectly cooked dishes.

Patience is Key: Smoking and grilling take time, so be patient and avoid constantly opening the lid to check on your food. Each time you open the lid, you release heat and smoke, affecting cooking times and results.

Brining and Marinating: Brining meats before smoking can help keep them moist and add flavour. Marinating is another great way to infuse flavour into your ingredients. Experiment with different brines and marinades to find your favourite combinations.

Resting: Allow your cooked meats to rest before slicing or serving. Resting allows the juices to redistribute, resulting in juicier and more flavorful meat.

Experimentation: Don't be afraid to try new techniques and recipes. BBQ is as much about creativity as it is about tradition. Experiment with ingredients, seasonings, and cooking methods to develop your signature style.

Cleanliness: Keep your grill and smoker clean to prevent flare-ups and ensure optimal performance. Remove ash and grease buildup regularly and clean the grates after each use.

Safety First: Always follow safety precautions when working with fire and hot surfaces. Use long-handled tools to avoid burns, and keep a fire extinguisher nearby.

By incorporating these expert tips and techniques into your BBQ repertoire, you'll be well on your way to mastering the art of smoking and grilling like a pro. Enjoy the journey and savour the delicious results!

PROVEN METHODS FOR ACHIEVING THE IDEAL SMOKE AND TEMPERATURE CONTROL.

Achieving the ideal smoke and temperature control is essential for delicious barbecue results. Here are some proven methods that you might find in the "Traeger Grill & Smoker Cookbook":

Start with a Clean Grill: Ensure your grill or smoker is clean before each use. Remove any ash, residue, or leftover charcoal from previous sessions. A clean grill promotes better airflow and temperature control.

Use High-Quality Fuel: Choose high-quality charcoal, wood pellets, or wood chunks for your grill or smoker. Inferior fuel can affect temperature stability and impart undesirable flavours to your food.

Mastering the Fire:

1. Learn to build and maintain a steady fire.

2. Whether you're using charcoal or wood pellets, arrange them to promote even burning and consistent heat output.

3. Use a chimney starter for charcoal grills to ensure uniform ignition.

Manage Airflow: Understand how airflow affects temperature control. Most grills and smokers have vents or dampers that allow you to regulate airflow. Open vents increase oxygen flow, raising the temperature, while closing vents reduce airflow and lower the temperature.

Utilize the "Minion Method": This method involves layering unlit charcoal with a small amount of lit charcoal to maintain a steady temperature over an extended period. It's particularly useful for long smoking sessions.

Water Pans and Thermal Mass: Place a water pan or thermal mass inside your grill or smoker, such as a ceramic plate or stone. These help regulate temperature fluctuations by absorbing and radiating heat evenly.

Monitor Temperature: Invest in a reliable thermometer to monitor both the grill's temperature and the internal temperature of your food. Wireless thermometers with remote monitoring capabilities allow you to monitor temperatures without constantly opening the lid.

Adjusting Fuel and Ventilation: Fine-tune your temperature control by adjusting the amount of fuel and airflow. If the temperature is too high, reduce the airflow or add fewer fuel sources. Conversely, increasing airflow or adding more fuel if the temperature is too low.

Wind and Weather Considerations: Be mindful of external factors like wind and weather conditions, as they can affect temperature control. Position your grill or smoker in a sheltered area or use windbreaks to minimize their impact.

Practice and Patience: Perfect smoke and temperature control requires practice and patience. Don't be discouraged by setbacks; use them as learning opportunities to refine your technique.

By implementing these proven methods and techniques, you'll be better equipped to achieve the ideal smoke and temperature control for consistently delicious barbecue results. Experimentation and experience will ultimately fine-tune your skills and elevate your BBQ game.

TROUBLESHOOTING TIPS AND ADVICE FOR OVERCOMING COMMON BBQ CHALLENGES.

Challenges can arise when it comes to BBQ, but with the right troubleshooting tips and advice, you can overcome them and still achieve fantastic results. Here are some common BBQ challenges and how to address them, as you might find in the "Traeger Grill & Smoker Cookbook":

Uneven Cooking: If your food is cooking unevenly, it could be due to hot spots on the grill. Rotate your food regularly to ensure even cooking, or consider investing in a grill with better heat distribution. You can also adjust the placement of the food on the grill to take advantage of cooler or hotter areas.

Dry or Tough Meat: Dry or tough meat often results from overcooking or cooking at too high a temperature. Use a meat thermometer to ensure your meat reaches the correct internal temperature without overcooking. Additionally, consider using a marinade or brine to help keep the meat moist during cooking.

Flare-Ups: Flare-ups occur when fat drips onto the flames, causing sudden bursts of high heat. To prevent flare-ups, trim excess fat from your meat before cooking, and keep a spray bottle of water nearby to quickly extinguish any flames. You can also move the food to a cooler part of the grill until the flare-up subsides.

Temperature Fluctuations: Inconsistent temperatures can result from poor airflow, inadequate fuel, or external factors like wind or weather. Ensure proper ventilation and fuel distribution in your grill or smoker, and consider using windbreaks to shield your cooking area from the elements. Regularly monitor and adjust the temperature as needed to maintain consistency.

Sticky or Stuck-on Food: Sticky or stuck-on food can be frustrating, especially when trying to flip or remove it from the grill. To prevent this, ensure your grill grates are clean and well-oiled before cooking. Use a grill brush to remove any residue between uses, and consider using a non-stick cooking spray or oiling the grates before adding food.

Smoke Flavors: While smoke is essential for BBQ flavour, excessive or unpleasant smoke flavours can overpower the taste of your food. Use high-quality wood pellets or chunks; avoid using green or overly resinous wood. Additionally, ensure proper ventilation and airflow in your grill or smoker to prevent the buildup of stale or acrid smoke.

Timing Issues: Timing is crucial in BBQ, especially when cooking multiple dishes or serving a large group. Plan and create a cooking schedule to ensure everything finishes cooking simultaneously. Use timers and alarms to remind you when to check or flip your food, and be prepared to adjust your schedule as needed based on temperature fluctuations or other factors.

Resting Periods: Resting meat after cooking allows the juices to redistribute, resulting in juicier and more flavorful meat. If you're short on time, it can be tempting to skip this step, but doing so can lead to dry or less flavorful meat. Plan and factor in sufficient resting time when scheduling your BBQ sessions.

By implementing these troubleshooting tips and advice, you'll be better equipped to overcome common BBQ challenges and achieve delicious results every time. Remember to stay patient and flexible, and don't be afraid to experiment to find what works best for you and your grill.

SMOKED BACON AND EGG BREAKFAST BURRITOS

Cooking Time: 20 minutes
 Servings: 4
Ingredients:

- Eight strips of smoked bacon

- Four large eggs

- 1/2 cup shredded cheddar cheese

- Four large flour tortillas

- One tablespoon olive oil

- Salt and pepper to taste

- Optional toppings: salsa, diced avocado, chopped cilantro

Directions:

1. cook the bacon until crispy in a large skillet over medium heat. R move it from the skillet and drain on paper towels. Once cooled, crumble the bacon into small pieces and set aside.

2 Add olive oil to the same skillet and heat over medium heat. Crack the eggs into the skillet and cook to your desired doneness, seasoning with salt and pepper.

3 Warm the tortillas in the skillet or microwave until soft and pliable.

4 To assemble the burritos, divide the scrambled eggs among the tortillas, placing them in the centre. Top each with crumbled bacon and shredded cheese.

5 Fold the sides of the tortillas over the filling, then roll them up tightly into burritos.

6 Serve immediately, or if making ahead, wrap each burrito in aluminium foil and store in the refrigerator for up to 2 days.

7 Optional: Unwrap the burritos from the foil before serving and reheat in the microwave for 1-2 minutes or until heated.

8 Serve with your favourite toppings, such as salsa, diced avocado, or chopped cilantro.

Nutrition (per serving):

- Calories: 420

- Total Fat: 27g

- Saturated Fat: 10g

- Cholesterol: 230mg

- Sodium: 830mg

- Total Carbohydrates: 23g

- Dietary Fiber: 1g

- Sugars: 1g

- Protein: 21g

MAPLE GLAZED SMOKED SAUSAGE BREAKFAST SKEWERS

Cooking Time: 20 minutes
Servings: 4
Ingredients:

- One package of smoked sausage (12 ounces), sliced into 1-inch pieces

- 1/4 cup maple syrup

- One tablespoon Dijon mustard

- One tablespoon olive oil

- Salt and pepper to taste

- One bell pepper, cut into chunks

- One red onion, cut into chunks

- Eight cherry tomatoes

- Wooden skewers, soaked in water for 30 minutes

Directions:

1 Preheat your grill or grill pan to medium-high heat.

2 whisk together the maple syrup, Dijon mustard, olive oil, salt, and pepper in a small bowl.

3 Alternately thread the sliced sausage, bell pepper chunks, red onion chunks, and cherry tomatoes onto the soaked wooden skewers.

4 Brush the skewers with the maple syrup mixture, coating all sides.

5 Place the skewers on the preheated grill and cook for 8-10 minutes, occasionally turning until the sausage is heated and the vegetables are tender and slightly charred.

6 Remove the skewers from the grill and brush with any remaining maple syrup mixture before serving.

Nutrition (per serving):

- Calories: 280

- Total Fat: 17g

- Saturated Fat: 5g

- Cholesterol: 35mg

- Sodium: 650mg

- Total Carbohydrate: 20g

- Dietary Fiber: 2g

- Sugars: 14g

- Protein: 12g

TRAEGER GRILLED FRENCH TOAST

Cooking Time: 20 minutes
Servings: 4
Ingredients:

- Eight slices of thick-cut bread (such as brioche or challah)

- Four large eggs

- 1 cup whole milk

- One teaspoon vanilla extract

- 1/2 teaspoon ground cinnamon

- 1/4 teaspoon ground nutmeg

- Two tablespoons unsalted butter, melted

- Maple syrup for serving

- Fresh berries, for garnish (optional)

- Powdered sugar for dusting (optional)

Directions:

1 Preheat your Traeger grill to 350°F (175°C) according to manufacturer instructions.

2. whisk together eggs, milk, vanilla extract, cinnamon, and nutmeg until well combined in a shallow dish.

3 Dip each slice of bread into the egg mixture, allowing it to soak for about 20-30 seconds on each side.

4 Brush the grill grates lightly with melted butter to prevent sticking.

5 Place the soaked bread slices directly onto the preheated grill. Close the lid and cook on each side for 3-4 minutes until golden brown is cooked through.

6 transfer the grilled French toast slices to a serving platter.

7 Serve hot with maple syrup drizzled on top. If desired, garnish with fresh berries and a dusting of powdered sugar.

8 Enjoy your Traeger Grilled French Toast!

Nutrition:

- Calories: 320 kcal
- Total Fat: 14g
- Saturated Fat: 7g
- Cholesterol: 210mg
- Sodium: 350mg
- Total Carbohydrates: 35g
- Dietary Fiber: 2g
- Sugars: 8g
- Protein: 13g

SMOKED BREAKFAST CASSEROLE WITH HASH BROWNS

Cooking Time: 1 hour 30 minutes

Servings: 8

Ingredients:

- 1 pound smoked sausage, diced
- One onion, chopped
- One red bell pepper, chopped
- One green bell pepper, chopped
- 1 (32-ounce) package of frozen hash brown potatoes, thawed
- 2 cups shredded cheddar cheese
- Eight large eggs
- 1 cup milk
- Salt and pepper to taste
- Cooking spray

Directions:

1 Preheat your oven to 350°F (175°C) Grease a 9x13 inch baking dish with cooking spray.

2 In a large skillet, cook the smoked sausage over medium heat until browned. Add chopped onion, red bell pepper, and green bell pepper. Cook until vegetables are tender, about 5 minutes. Remove from heat and set aside.

3. Combine the thawed hash brown potatoes, cooked sausage and vegetable mixture, and shredded cheddar cheese in a large bowl. Mix well and spread evenly into the prepared baking dish.

4 In another bowl, whisk together the eggs and milk. Season with salt and pepper to taste. Pour the egg mixture over the hash brown mixture into the baking dish.

5 Bake in the oven for 45-50 minutes until the centre is set and the edges are golden brown.

6 Allow the casserole to cool for a few minutes before slicing and serving.

7 Serve hot and enjoy your delicious Smoked Breakfast Casserole with Hash Browns!

Nutrition:

- **Calories:** 420 kcal
- **Total Fat:** 28g
  - **Saturated Fat:** 12g
  - **Trans Fat:** 0g
- **Cholesterol:** 260mg
- **Sodium:** 650mg
- **Total Carbohydrates:** 20g
  - **Dietary Fiber:** 2g
  - **Sugars:** 3g
- **Protein:** 22g

APPLEWOOD SMOKED BREAKFAST PIZZA

Cooking Time: 30 minutes
Servings: 4
Ingredients:

- One pre-made pizza dough
- 1 cup shredded mozzarella cheese
- Four slices applewood smoked bacon, cooked and crumbled
- Four large eggs
- 1/2 cup diced red bell pepper
- 1/4 cup chopped green onions
- Salt and pepper to taste
- Olive oil for brushing

Directions:

1 Preheat your oven to 425°F (220°C).

2 Roll out the pizza dough on a lightly floured surface to your desired thickness.

3 Place the rolled-out dough onto a baking sheet lined with parchment paper.

4 Brush the surface of the dough with olive oil.

5 Sprinkle half of the shredded mozzarella cheese evenly over the dough.

Six evenly Distribute the cooked and crumbled bacon, diced red bell pepper, and chopped green onions over the cheese.

7 Carefully crack the eggs onto the pizza, evenly spacing them.

8 Sprinkle the remaining mozzarella cheese over the top of the pizza.

9 Season with salt and pepper to taste.

10. Place the pizza in the oven and bake for 15-20 minutes until the crust is golden brown and the eggs are set.

11. Once done, remove the pizza from the oven and let it cool for a few minutes before slicing.

12. Slice the pizza into wedges and serve hot.

Nutrition:

- **Calories:** 380 kcal
- **Total Fat:** 18g
- **Saturated Fat:** 7g
- **Cholesterol:** 205mg
- **Sodium:** 700mg
- **Total Carbohydrates:** 33g
- **Dietary Fiber:** 2g
- **Sugars:** 2g
- **Protein:** 20g

GRILLED BREAKFAST QUESADILLAS WITH HAM AND CHEESE

Cooking Time: 15 minutes
Servings: 4
Ingredients:

- Eight large flour tortillas
- 1 cup diced cooked ham
- 1 cup shredded cheddar cheese
- 1 cup shredded mozzarella cheese
- Four large eggs
- 1/4 cup milk
- Salt and pepper to taste
- Two tablespoons butter
- Salsa, sour cream, and sliced avocado for serving (optional)

Directions:

1 whisk the eggs, milk, salt, and pepper in a mixing bowl until well combined.

2 Heat a large skillet over medium heat and melt one tablespoon of butter.

3 Pour the egg mixture into the skillet and cook, stirring occasionally, until the eggs are scrambled and cooked. Remove from heat and set aside.

4 Layout 4 of the tortillas on a flat surface. Divide the scrambled eggs evenly among the tortillas, spreading them in an even layer.

5 Top the eggs with diced ham, shredded cheddar, and mozzarella cheese.

6 Place the remaining four tortillas on the filling to create quesadillas.

7 Heat a grill pan or skillet over medium heat and melt the remaining butter.

8 Carefully place the quesadillas onto the grill pan or skillet and cook for 2-3 minutes on each side until the tortillas are golden brown and crispy and the cheese is melted.

9 Remove the quesadillas from the heat and let them cool slightly before cutting into wedges.

10. Serve the grilled breakfast quesadillas with salsa, sour cream, and sliced avocado if desired.

Nutrition:

- Calories: 430
- Total Fat: 24g
- Saturated Fat: 12g
- Cholesterol: 220mg

- Sodium: 970mg
- Total Carbohydrates: 29g
- Dietary Fiber: 2g
- Sugars: 1g
- Protein: 23g

TRAEGER SMOKED AVOCADO TOAST WITH POACHED EGGS

Cooking Time: 30 minutes
Servings: 4
Ingredients:

- Four large eggs
- Two ripe avocados
- Four slices of whole-grain bread
- One lemon, juiced
- One tablespoon olive oil
- Salt and pepper to taste
- Optional toppings: sliced cherry tomatoes, red pepper flakes, chopped cilantro

Directions:

1 **Preheat the Traeger Grill:** Preheat your Traeger grill to 225°F (107°C) using oak pellets for a subtle smoky flavour.

2 **Prepare the Avocado Mixture:** Cut the avocados in half, remove the pits, and scoop the flesh into a bowl. Mash the avocado with a fork until smooth. Add lemon juice, olive oil, salt, and pepper to taste. Mix well and set aside.

3 **Toast the Bread:** Place the slices of whole grain bread directly on the grill grates. Close the lid and toast for about 5-7 minutes or until the bread is lightly browned and crispy.

4 **Poach the Eggs:** Bring a pot of water to a simmer while the bread is toasting. Crack each egg into a small cup or ramekin. Gently slide the eggs, one at a time, into the simmering water. Poach for 3-4 minutes until the whites are set but the yolks are still runny. Remove the poached eggs with a slotted spoon and place them on a plate lined with paper towels to drain excess water.

5 **Assemble the Avocado Toast:** Spread a generous amount of the mashed avocado mixture onto each slice of toasted bread. Top each toast with a poached egg.

6 **Add Optional Toppings:** For extra flavour and colour, garnish the avocado toast with optional toppings such as sliced cherry tomatoes, red pepper flakes, or chopped cilantro.

7 Keep the Traeger Smoked Avocado Toast with Poached Eggs immediately while warm. Enjoy your delicious and nutritious breakfast or brunch!

Nutrition (per serving):
CALORIES: 320
TOTAL FAT: 20g
SATURATED FAT: 3g

CHOLESTEROL: 185mg
SODIUM: 300mg
TOTAL CARBOHYDRATES: 25g
DIETARY FIBER: 10g
PROTEIN: 12g

SMOKED SALMON BAGEL SANDWICHES

Cooking Time: 10 minutes
 Servings: 2
Ingredients:

- Two bagels, sliced
- 150g smoked salmon
- Four tablespoons cream cheese
- One tablespoon capers, drained
- One small red onion, thinly sliced
- One tablespoon fresh dill, chopped
- One tablespoon lemon juice
- Salt and black pepper to taste

Directions:
1 **Prepare the Bagels:** Toast the bagel slices until golden brown and crisp.
2 **Assemble the Sandwiches:** Spread a generous layer of cream cheese on each half of the toasted bagels.
3 **Add Smoked Salmon:** Divide the smoked salmon evenly between the bagel halves and place it on the cream cheese.
4 **Add Toppings:** Sprinkle capers, red onion slices, and chopped dill over the smoked salmon.
5 **Season:** Drizzle lemon juice over the toppings and season with salt and black pepper according to taste.
6 **Assemble the Sandwiches:** Place the other half of the bagel on top to form a sandwich.
7 Serve immediately and enjoy your delicious smoked salmon bagel sandwiches!
Nutrition:

- CALORIES: Approximately 320 per serving
- PROTEIN: 20g
- CARBOHYDRATES: 32g
- FAT: 12g
- SATURATED FAT: 4g
- CHOLESTEROL: 25mg
- SODIUM: 780mg
- FIBER: 2g
- SUGAR: 2g
- VITAMIN D: 0.5mcg
- CALCIUM: 70mg
- IRON: 2mg
- POTASSIUM: 220mg

WOOD-FIRED BREAKFAST FRITTATA

Cooking Time: 25 minutes
Servings: 4
Ingredients:

- Eight large eggs
- 1/4 cup milk
- 1 cup chopped spinach
- 1/2 cup diced bell peppers (red, yellow, or green)
- 1/2 cup diced onions
- 1/2 cup diced mushrooms
- 1/2 cup diced tomatoes
- 1/2 cup shredded cheddar cheese

- Salt and pepper to taste
- Olive oil for greasing

Directions:

1 **Prepare the Fire:** Start your wood-fired oven and let it preheat to about 375°F (190°C). Ensure you have a good bed of embers for even cooking.

2 **Prepare Ingredients:** In a bowl, whisk together the eggs and milk until well combined. Season with salt and pepper. Set aside. Chop all your vegetables and have them ready.

3 **Sauté Vegetables:** Heat a skillet over medium heat and add olive oil. Add onions, bell peppers, and mushrooms. Sauté until softened, about 3-4 minutes. Add spinach and tomatoes. Cook until spinach is wilted, about 1-2 minutes more. Remove from heat.

4 **Assemble Frittata:** Grease a cast-iron skillet or a baking dish with olive oil. Spread the sautéed vegetables evenly on the bottom. Sprinkle shredded cheddar cheese over the vegetables.

5 **Pour Egg Mixture:** Pour the egg and milk mixture over the vegetables and cheese, ensuring everything is evenly coated.

6 **Cook in a Wood-Fired Oven:** Place the skillet or baking dish in the wood-fired oven. Bake for 15-20 minutes or until the frittata is set and the top is golden brown.

7 **Serve:** Once cooked, remove the frittata from the oven and let it cool for a few minutes before slicing. Serve hot, garnished with fresh herbs if desired.

Nutrition:

- **Calories:** 235 kcal
- **Protein:** 17g
- **Carbohydrates:** 8g
- **Fat:** 15g
- **Saturated Fat:** 6g
- **Cholesterol:** 384mg
- **Sodium:** 389mg
- **Potassium:** 372mg
- **Fiber:** 2g
- **Sugar:** 4g
- **Vitamin A:** 2555IU
- **Vitamin C:** 40mg
- **Calcium:** 226mg
- **Iron:** 2mg

BBQ BREAKFAST SLIDERS WITH EGG AND CHEESE

Cooking Time: 25 minutes
Servings: 6 sliders
Ingredients:

- Six slider buns
- Six large eggs
- Six slices of cheddar cheese
- Six slices of cooked bacon
- 1/2 cup of your favourite BBQ sauce
- Salt and pepper to taste
- Butter for greasing the pan

Directions:

1 Preheat your oven to 350°F (175°C).

2 In a skillet over medium heat, cook the bacon until crispy. Set aside on a paper towel-lined plate to drain excess grease.

3 Grease a baking dish with butter and place the bottom halves of the slider buns in the dish.

4 Crack an egg onto each bun bottom. Season with salt and pepper to taste.

5 Bake in the oven for 10-12 minutes or until the eggs are set.

6 Remove the dish from the oven and place a slice of cheddar cheese on top of each egg.

7 Lay a slice of bacon on top of the cheese.

8 Drizzle BBQ sauce over the bacon.

9 Place the top halves of the slider buns on top of each sandwich.

10. Return the dish to the oven and bake for 5 minutes until the cheese is melted and the sliders are heated through.

11. Serve hot and enjoy your BBQ breakfast sliders!

Nutrition: (Note: Nutritional values may vary depending on specific ingredients.)

- Calories: Approximately 350 per slider
- Protein: Approximately 15g per slider
- Fat: Approximately 20g per slider
- Carbohydrates: Approximately 25g per slider
- Fiber: Approximately 1g per slider

TRAEGER GRILLED BANANA PANCAKES

Cooking Time: 20 minutes

Servings: 4

Ingredients:

- Two large ripe bananas
- 2 cups all-purpose flour
- Two tablespoons granulated sugar
- Two teaspoons baking powder
- 1/2 teaspoon salt

- 1 1/2 cups milk
- Two large eggs
- Two tablespoons melted butter
- Cooking spray or additional butter for grilling
- Maple syrup and sliced bananas for serving (optional)

Directions:

1 Preheat your Traeger grill to 375°F (190°C).

2 mash the ripe bananas with a fork until smooth in a large mixing bowl.

3 whisk together the flour, sugar, baking powder, and salt in another bowl.

4 Add the milk, eggs, and melted butter to the mashed bananas and whisk until well combined.

5 Gradually add the dry ingredients to the wet ingredients, stirring until combined. Be careful not to overmix; some lumps are okay.

6 Grease the grates of your Traeger grill with cooking spray or butter.

7 Pour about 1/4 cup of batter onto the grill for each pancake, spreading it slightly with the back of a spoon to form circles.

8 Close the grill and cook the pancakes for 2-3 minutes, or until bubbles form on the surface and the edges begin to set.

9 Carefully flip the pancakes using a spatula and cook for 2-3 minutes until golden brown and cooked through.

10. Remove the pancakes from the grill and repeat with the remaining batter, greasing the grates as needed.

11. Serve the Traeger grilled banana pancakes warm with maple syrup and sliced bananas if desired.

Nutrition: NOTE: NUTRITION INFORMATION IS APPROXIMATE AND MAY VARY DEPENDING ON SPECIFIC INGREDIENTS.

- Calories: 320 kcal
- Total Fat: 8g
- Saturated Fat: 4g
- Cholesterol: 95mg
- Sodium: 520mg
- Total Carbohydrates: 55g
- Dietary Fiber: 3g
- Sugars: 14g
- Protein: 9g

BACON-WRAPPED STUFFED BREAKFAST PEPPERS

Cooking Time: 35 minutes

Servings: 4

Ingredients:

- Four large bell peppers (any colour), halved and seeds removed
- Eight slices of bacon
- Six large eggs
- 1/4 cup milk
- 1/2 cup shredded cheddar cheese
- 1/4 cup diced onion
- 1/4 cup diced bell peppers (any colour)
- Salt and pepper to taste
- Chopped fresh parsley for garnish (optional)

Directions:

1 Preheat your oven to 375°F (190°C).

Two. Whisk together the eggs, milk, shredded cheese, diced onion, bell peppers, salt, and pepper in a bowl.

3 Place the halved bell peppers on a baking sheet lined with parchment paper, cut side up.

4 Carefully fill each bell pepper half with the egg mixture until they are almost full.

5 Wrap each stuffed pepper half with a slice of bacon, securing it around the pepper.

6 Place the bacon-wrapped stuffed peppers in the oven and bake for 25-30 minutes until the bacon is crispy and the eggs are set.

7 Once cooked, remove from the oven and let them cool for a few minutes.

8 Garnish with chopped fresh parsley if desired, then serve hot and enjoy!

Nutrition (per serving):

- Calories: 320
- Total Fat: 21g
- Saturated Fat: 8g
- Cholesterol: 280mg
- Sodium: 580mg
- Total Carbohydrates: 10g
- Dietary Fiber: 2g
- Sugars: 5g
- Protein: 22g

SMOKED BREAKFAST HASH WITH SWEET POTATOES

Cooking Time: 30 minutes

Servings: 4

Ingredients:

- Two large sweet potatoes, peeled and diced
- One tablespoon olive oil
- One onion, diced
- Two cloves garlic, minced
- One bell pepper, diced
- 1 cup diced cooked smoked sausage or bacon
- Salt and pepper to taste
- Four eggs
- Chopped fresh parsley for garnish (optional)

Directions:

1 Heat the olive oil in a large skillet over medium heat. Add the diced sweet potatoes and cook for about 10-12 minutes, stirring occasionally, until golden and tender.

2 Add the diced onion, minced garlic, and bell pepper to the skillet. Cook for an additional 5 minutes until the vegetables are softened.

3 Stir in the diced smoked sausage or bacon, and season with salt and pepper to taste. Cook for another 3-5 minutes until everything is heated through.

4 Using a spoon, create four wells in the hash mixture. Crack an egg into each well. Cover the skillet and cook for about 5-7 minutes, or until the eggs are cooked to your desired level of doneness.

5 Once the eggs are cooked, garnish the hash with chopped fresh parsley if desired. Serve hot and enjoy!

Nutrition:

- Calories: 320 kcal
- Fat: 15g
- Carbohydrates: 28g
- Fiber: 4g
- Protein: 18g
- Sodium: 570mg

GRILLED BLUEBERRY MUFFINS WITH STREUSEL TOPPING

Cooking Time: 20 minutes
 Servings: 12 muffins
Ingredients:
For the muffins:

- 2 cups all-purpose flour
- 1/2 cup granulated sugar
- Two teaspoons baking powder

- 1/2 teaspoon salt

- 1/2 cup unsalted butter, melted

- Two large eggs

- 1 cup milk

- One teaspoon vanilla extract

- 1 1/2 cups fresh blueberries

For the streusel topping:

- 1/4 cup all-purpose flour

- 1/4 cup granulated sugar

- Two tablespoons unsalted butter, cold and diced

- 1/2 teaspoon ground cinnamon

Directions:

1 Preheat your grill to medium heat, around 350°F (175°C).

2 Whisk the flour, sugar, baking powder, and salt in a large mixing bowl.

3 mix the melted butter, eggs, milk, and vanilla extract in a separate bowl until well combined.

4 Pour the wet ingredients into the dry ingredients and stir until combined. Be careful not to overmix. Gently fold in the blueberries.

5 Line a muffin tin with paper liners and fill about two-thirds with the muffin batter in each cup.

6 In a small bowl, Combine the streusel topping ingredients—flour, sugar, cold butter, and cinnamon. Use a fork or pastry cutter to cut the butter into the dry ingredients until it crumbles.

7 Sprinkle the streusel topping evenly over the muffin batter in the muffin tin.

8 Place the muffin tin on the preheated grill and close the lid. Grill for about 15-18 minutes or until a toothpick inserted into the centre of a muffin comes out clean.

9 Once cooked, remove the muffins from the grill and let them cool in the tin for a few minutes before transferring to a wire rack to cool completely.

10. Serve the grilled blueberry muffins warm or at room temperature, and enjoy!

Nutrition: (PER SERVING)

- Calories: 235

- Total Fat: 10g

- Saturated Fat: 6g

- Cholesterol: 52mg

- Sodium: 204mg

- Total Carbohydrate: 33g

- Dietary Fiber: 1g

- Sugars: 14g

- Protein: 4g

SAUSAGE AND EGG BREAKFAST BOMBS

Cooking Time: 25 minutes
Servings: 4
Ingredients:

- Eight large eggs
- Eight breakfast sausage links
- One can refrigerated biscuit dough
- 1 cup shredded cheddar cheese
- Salt and pepper to taste
- Optional: chopped chives or green onions for garnish

Directions:

1 Preheat your oven to 375°F (190°C). Line a baking sheet with parchment paper or lightly grease it with cooking spray.

2 In a medium-sized bowl, beat the eggs together and season with salt and pepper to taste.

3 Heat a skillet over medium heat and cook the breakfast sausage links until they are browned and cooked about 8-10 minutes. Remove from the skillet and let them cool slightly.

4 roll out the biscuit dough on a clean surface while the sausage cools. Flatten each biscuit with your hands or a rolling pin until it's about ¼ inch thick.

5 Place a cooked sausage link in the centre of each flattened biscuit. Sprinkle some shredded cheese over the sausage.

6 Carefully fold the biscuit dough around the sausage and cheese, sealing it tightly so no filling leaks.

7 Place the filled biscuit bombs seam-side down on the prepared baking sheet.

8 Brush the tops of the bombs with the beaten egg mixture for a golden finish.

9 Bake in the oven for 12-15 minutes or until the biscuits are golden brown and cooked.

10. Once baked, remove from the oven and let cool for a few minutes before serving.

11. Optionally, garnish with chopped chives or green onions before serving.

Nutrition:

- Calories: 420 kcal
- Fat: 28g
- Carbohydrates: 21g
- Protein: 22g
- Fiber: 1g
- Sugar: 2g
- Sodium: 820mg

TRAEGER SMOKED OMELETTE WITH SPINACH AND FETA

Cooking Time: 25 minutes

Servings: 2
Ingredients:

- Six large eggs
- 1 cup fresh spinach leaves, chopped
- 1/4 cup crumbled feta cheese
- 1/4 cup diced tomatoes
- 1/4 cup diced onions
- 1/4 cup diced bell peppers
- Salt and pepper to taste
- Cooking spray or olive oil

Directions:

1 Preheat your Traeger smoker to 350°F (175°C).

2 In a bowl, crack the eggs and beat them lightly with a fork or whisk. Season with salt and pepper to taste.

3 Lightly grease a cast-iron skillet with cooking spray or olive oil.

4 Spread the chopped spinach evenly on the bottom of the skillet.

5 Sprinkle the diced tomatoes, onions, and bell peppers over the spinach.

6 Pour the beaten eggs over the vegetables in the skillet.

7 Place the skillet on the preheated Traeger smoker and close the lid.

8 Smoke the omelette for about 20-25 minutes or until the eggs are set and cooked.

9 Sprinkle the crumbled feta cheese over the cooked omelette.

10. Using a spatula, carefully fold the omelette in half.

11. Transfer the smoked omelette to a serving plate and serve hot.

Nutrition:

- PER SERVING (1/2 OF RECIPE):
    - Calories: 220
    - Total Fat: 14g
    - Saturated Fat: 5g
    - Cholesterol: 435mg
    - Sodium: 330mg
    - Total Carbohydrates: 5g
    - Dietary Fiber: 1g
    - Sugars: 2g
    - Protein: 17g

MAPLE BOURBON GLAZED BREAKFAST SAUSAGE

Cooking Time: 20 minutes
Servings: 4
Ingredients:

- 1 pound breakfast sausages
- Two tablespoons maple syrup
- Two tablespoons bourbon
- One tablespoon brown sugar
- One teaspoon Dijon mustard
- 1/4 teaspoon ground black pepper
- Pinch of salt
- One tablespoon olive oil

Directions:

1 In a small bowl, whisk together maple syrup, bourbon, brown sugar, Dijon mustard, black pepper, and salt until well combined to make the glaze.

2 Heat olive oil in a large skillet over medium-high heat. Add the sausages and cook for 8-10 minutes, turning occasionally, until browned and cooked.

3 Once the sausages are cooked, reduce the heat to medium and pour the glaze over the sausages in the skillet.

4 Continue cooking, turning the sausages occasionally for another 5-7 minutes, allowing the glaze to thicken and coat the sausages evenly.

5 Once the sausages are nicely glazed and the sauce has thickened, remove them from the skillet and transfer to a serving platter.

6 Serve the Maple Bourbon Glazed Breakfast Sausages hot, garnished with fresh herbs if desired.

Nutrition:

- **Calories:** 320 kcal
- **Fat:** 24g
- **Saturated Fat:** 8g
- **Cholesterol:** 60mg
- **Sodium:** 720mg
- **Carbohydrates:** 8g
- **Fibre:** 0g
- **Sugar:** 7g
- **Protein:** 14g

GRILLED BREAKFAST TACOS WITH CHORIZO AND EGGS

Cooking Time: 20 minutes
Servings: 4
Ingredients:

- Eight small flour tortillas
- 8 ounces chorizo sausage, casing removed

- Six large eggs
- 1/2 cup shredded cheddar cheese
- 1/4 cup diced red onion
- 1/4 cup chopped fresh cilantro
- Salt and pepper to taste
- Cooking spray

Directions:

1 Preheat your grill to medium-high heat.

2 In a skillet over medium heat, cook the chorizo sausage until browned and cooked through, breaking it apart with a spoon as it cooks.

3 While the chorizo cooks, crack the eggs into a bowl and whisk them together until well beaten.

4 Once the chorizo is cooked, push it to one side of the skillet and pour the beaten eggs into the empty side.

5 Scramble the eggs until fully cooked, and then mix them with the chorizo.

6 Remove the skillet from the heat and stir in the shredded cheddar cheese until melted.

7 Spray the grill lightly with cooking spray to prevent sticking.

8 Place the flour tortillas directly on the grill grates and cook for about 30 seconds to 1 minute on each side until they are lightly toasted and have grill marks.

9 Remove the tortillas from the grill and divide the chorizo and egg mixture evenly.

10. Top each taco with diced red onion and chopped cilantro.

11. Season with salt and pepper to taste.

12. Serve immediately and enjoy!

Nutrition (per serving):

- Calories: 390
- Total Fat: 23g
- Saturated Fat: 9g
- Cholesterol: 290mg
- Sodium: 870mg
- Total Carbohydrate: 25g
- Dietary Fiber: 2g
- Sugars: 1g
- Protein: 21g

SMOKED BREAKFAST SAUSAGE BREAKFAST BISCUITS

Cooking Time: 30 minutes

Servings: 4

Ingredients:

- 8 smoked breakfast sausage links

- 1 cup all-purpose flour
- One tablespoon baking powder
- 1/2 teaspoon salt
- 1/4 cup cold unsalted butter, diced
- 1/2 cup milk
- Four slices cheddar cheese
- Four large eggs
- Salt and pepper to taste
- Optional: Maple syrup or hot sauce for serving

Directions:

1 Preheat your oven to 400°F (200°C).

2 In a skillet over medium heat, cook the smoked breakfast sausage links until they are browned and fully cooked, about 8-10 minutes. Once done, set them aside on a plate lined with paper towels to absorb excess grease.

3. Combine the all-purpose flour, baking powder, and salt in a large mixing bowl. Add the diced cold butter to the flour mixture, and use a pastry cutter or your fingertips to work the butter into the flour until the mixture resembles coarse crumbs.

4 Slowly pour in the milk and stir until a dough forms.

5 Turn the dough onto a lightly floured surface and knead it gently until it comes together. Roll the dough out to about 1/2-inch thickness.

6 Cut out eight dough rounds using a round biscuit cutter or the rim of a glass.

7 Place half the rounds onto a baking sheet lined with parchment paper. Top each round with a slice of cheddar cheese and a cooked sausage link. Cover each sausage with another dough round, pressing the edges together to seal.

8 Beat the eggs in a small bowl and season with salt and pepper to taste. Brush the tops of each biscuit with the beaten egg mixture.

9 Bake in the oven for 12-15 minutes until the biscuits are golden brown and cooked.

10. Serve the smoked breakfast sausage breakfast biscuits warm, optionally drizzled with maple syrup or accompanied by hot sauce for extra flavour.

Nutrition (per serving):

- Calories: 480
- Total Fat: 30g
- Saturated Fat: 14g
- Cholesterol: 245mg
- Sodium: 950mg
- Total Carbohydrate: 31g
- Dietary Fiber: 1g
- Sugars: 2g

- Protein: 22g

WOOD-FIRED BREAKFAST CROISSANTS WITH HAM AND CHEESE

Cooking Time: 20 minutes
Servings: 4
Ingredients:

- Four large croissants
- Eight slices of ham
- Four slices of Swiss cheese
- Four large eggs
- Salt and pepper to taste
- Two tablespoons butter, melted
- Optional: chopped chives or parsley for garnish

Directions:
1 Preheat your wood-fired oven to 375°F (190°C).
2 Slice each croissant horizontally, but not all through, creating a pocket for the filling.
3 Place two slices of ham and one slice of Swiss cheese inside each croissant.
4 Crack one egg into each croissant pocket. Season with salt and pepper.
5 Brush the outer surface of each croissant with melted butter.
6 Place the croissants directly onto the oven rack or a baking tray and bake in the wood-fired oven for about 15-18 minutes, until the croissants are golden brown and the eggs are set.
7 Remove the croissants from the oven and let them cool slightly before serving.
8 Garnish with chopped chives or parsley if desired. Serve warm.
Nutrition (per serving):

- Calories: 420
- Total Fat: 27g
- Saturated Fat: 14g
- Cholesterol: 225mg
- Sodium: 900mg
- Total Carbohydrates: 24g
- Dietary Fiber: 1g
- Sugars: 5g
- Protein: 20g

SMOKED BBQ CHICKEN SANDWICHES

Cooking Time: 4 hours
Servings: 4
Ingredients:

- Four boneless, skinless chicken breasts
- 1 cup BBQ sauce (your favourite brand)
- One tablespoon of olive oil
- One teaspoon of smoked paprika
- One teaspoon of garlic powder
- Salt and pepper to taste
- Four hamburger buns
- Optional toppings: sliced red onion, lettuce, tomato

Directions:

1. **Prepare the Chicken:** Preheat your smoker to 225°F (107°C). In a small bowl, mix olive oil, smoked paprika, garlic powder, salt, and pepper. Rub this mixture evenly over the chicken breasts.

2. **Smoke the Chicken:** Place the chicken breasts on the grates once the smoker is ready. Close the lid and smoke for 2-3 hours, or until the internal temperature of the chicken reaches 165°F (74°C) and the chicken is tender and juicy.

3. **Shred the Chicken:** Remove the smoked chicken breasts from the smoker and let them rest for a few minutes. Then, using two forks, shred the chicken into bite-sized pieces.

4. **Add BBQ Sauce:** In a large bowl, combine the shredded chicken with BBQ sauce, ensuring all the pieces are coated evenly.

5. **Assemble the Sandwiches:** Toast the hamburger buns lightly. Place a generous amount of the BBQ chicken mixture onto the bottom half of each bun. Add optional toppings like sliced red onion, lettuce, or tomato. Top with the other half of the bun.

6. **Serve:** Serve the smoked BBQ chicken sandwiches immediately, with your favourite sides like coleslaw or potato salad.

GRILLED VEGGIE WRAPS WITH PESTO MAYO

Cooking Time: 20 minutes
 Servings: 4
Ingredients:
For Grilled Veggies:

- Two large bell peppers, sliced

- One zucchini, sliced lengthwise

- One yellow squash sliced lengthwise

- One red onion, sliced

- 2 tablespoons olive oil

- Salt and pepper to taste

For Pesto Mayo:

- 1/2 cup mayonnaise

- Two tablespoons of prepared pesto sauce

For Wraps:

- Four large tortillas

- 1 cup baby spinach leaves

- 1 cup shredded mozzarella cheese

- Additional pesto sauce for drizzling (optional)

Directions:

1. **Preheat Grill:** Preheat your grill to medium-high heat.

2. **Prepare Veggies:** In a large bowl, toss sliced bell peppers, zucchini, yellow squash, red onion with olive oil, salt, and pepper until well coated.

3. **Grill Veggies:** Place the veggies on the preheated grill and cook for about 5-7 minutes on each side until they are tender and have grill marks.

4. **Make Pesto Mayo:** Mix mayonnaise and pesto sauce in a small bowl until well combined. Set aside.

5. **Assemble Wraps:** Lay out the tortillas and spread a generous spoonful of pesto mayo onto each tortilla.

6. **Layer Ingredients:** Layer each tortilla with grilled veggies, baby spinach leaves, and shredded mozzarella cheese.

7. **Wrap:** Fold the sides of the tortillas over the filling, then roll them up tightly.

8. **Serve:** Cut each wrap in half diagonally and serve immediately. If desired, drizzle additional pesto sauce on top before serving.

Nutrition (per serving):

NOTE: NUTRITIONAL VALUES MAY VARY DEPENDING ON SPECIFIC INGREDIENTS AND SERVING SIZE.

- Calories: 380

- Fat: 25g

- Saturated Fat: 6g

- Cholesterol: 25mg

- Sodium: 610mg

- Carbohydrates: 30g

- Fiber: 5g

- Sugar: 6g

- Protein: 10g

TRAEGER GRILLED CHEESEBURGERS WITH CARAMELIZED ONIONS

Cooking Time: 30 minutes

Servings: 4

Ingredients:

- 1 lb ground beef
- Four hamburger buns
- One large onion, thinly sliced
- Four slices of cheese (cheddar, American, or your choice)
- Two tablespoons of olive oil
- Salt and pepper to taste
- Optional toppings: lettuce, tomato, pickles, condiments of your choice

Directions:

1. **Prepare the Caramelized Onions:** Heat 1 tablespoon of olive oil in a skillet over medium heat. Add the thinly sliced onions and cook, stirring occasionally, until they become soft and golden brown, about 15-20 minutes—season with salt and pepper to taste. Set aside.

2. **Preheat the Grill:** Follow the manufacturer's instructions to heat your Traeger grill to 400°F (200°C).

3. **Form the Patties:** Divide the ground beef into four equal portions and shape them into burger patties—season both sides with salt and pepper.

4. **Grill the Patties:** Place the burger patties directly on the preheated grill grates. Cook for about 5-7 minutes on each side until they reach your desired level of doneness. During the last few minutes of grilling, add a slice of cheese on top of each patty and allow it to melt.

5. **Toast the Buns:** While the patties are grilling, lightly brush the hamburger buns with the remaining olive oil. Place them on the grill, cut side down, and toast for about 1-2 minutes until they are lightly golden brown.

6. **Assemble the Burgers:** Place a grilled burger patty on the bottom half of each bun. Top with a generous amount of caramelized onions. Add any additional toppings of your choice, such as lettuce, tomato, pickles, or condiments.

7. **Serve:** Close the burgers with the top half of the toasted buns and serve immediately.

Nutrition (per serving):

- Calories: 450
- Total Fat: 24g
- Saturated Fat: 8g
- Cholesterol: 80mg
- Sodium: 550mg
- Total Carbohydrate: 27g
- Dietary Fiber: 2g

- Sugars: 5g
- Protein: 30g

WOOD-FIRED CHICKEN CAESAR SALAD

Cooking Time: 30 minutes
Servings: 4
Ingredients:

- Four boneless, skinless chicken breasts
- One tablespoon of olive oil
- Salt and pepper to taste
- One large head of romaine lettuce, washed and chopped
- 1 cup cherry tomatoes, halved
- 1/2 cup freshly grated Parmesan cheese
- 1 cup croutons
- Caesar dressing (store-bought or homemade)
- Lemon wedges for garnish

Directions:

1. **Prepare the Grill:** Preheat your wood-fired grill to medium-high heat.

2. **Grill the Chicken:** Rub the chicken breasts with olive oil and generously season with salt and pepper. Place the chicken breasts on the preheated grill and cook for 6-7 minutes per side until the internal temperature reaches 165°F (75°C). Remove from the grill and let them rest for a few minutes before slicing.

3. **Assemble the Salad:** In a large bowl, combine chopped romaine lettuce, halved cherry tomatoes, grated Parmesan cheese, and croutons.

4. **Slice the Chicken:** Once rested, slice the grilled chicken breasts into thin strips.

5. **Dress the Salad:** Drizzle Caesar dressing over the salad ingredients and toss until everything is evenly coated.

6. **Serve:** Divide the salad among serving plates or bowls. Top each portion with sliced grilled chicken. Garnish with lemon wedges.

Nutrition (per serving):

- Calories: 350
- Total Fat: 15g
  - Saturated Fat: 4g
- Cholesterol: 90mg
- Sodium: 600mg
- Total Carbohydrates: 15g
  - Dietary Fiber: 3g
  - Sugars: 3g
- Protein: 40g

SMOKED PULLED PORK SLIDERS WITH COLESLAW

Cooking Time: 8 hours (plus additional time for marinating). **Servings:** 8-10

Ingredients:

- 4-5 pounds pork shoulder (also known as pork butt), bone-in or boneless
- 1 cup BBQ rub (store-bought or homemade)
- 1 cup apple cider vinegar
- 1 cup water
- 2 cups BBQ sauce
- 16-20 slider buns

For the Coleslaw:

- 4 cups shredded cabbage (green and purple mix)
- One carrot, grated
- 1/2 cup mayonnaise

- Two tablespoons of apple cider vinegar
- One tablespoon honey
- Salt and pepper to taste

Directions:

1. Prepare the Pork:

- Trim excess fat from the pork shoulder and rub it generously with the BBQ rub, covering all sides. Let it marinate in the refrigerator for at least 2 hours, preferably overnight.

2. Preheat the Smoker:

- Preheat your smoker to 225°F (110°C). Use your choice of wood chips (hickory, apple, or cherry) for smoking.

3. Smoke the Pork:

- Place the pork shoulder on the smoker rack and smoke it for about 6-8 hours, or until the internal temperature reaches 195-200°F (90-95°C) and the meat is tender and easily shreddable.

4. Make the Coleslaw:

- In a large bowl, combine the shredded cabbage and grated carrot.
- In a separate small bowl, whisk together the mayonnaise, apple cider vinegar, honey, salt, and pepper until well combined.
- Pour the dressing over the cabbage mixture and toss until evenly coated. Adjust seasoning if necessary. Cover and refrigerate until ready to use.

5. Pull the Pork:

- Once the pork is done, remove it from the smoker and rest for about 20-30 minutes. Then, shred the pork into bite-sized pieces using two forks or meat claws, discarding any excess fat.

6. Assemble the Sliders:

- Split the slider buns and lightly toast them on the smoker or grill.
- Place a generous amount of pulled pork onto the bottom half of each bun.
- Top the pork with a spoonful of BBQ sauce and a scoop of coleslaw.
- Place the top half of the bun on top and secure with a toothpick, if needed.

7. Serve and Enjoy:

- Arrange the sliders on a platter and serve them hot with extra BBQ sauce and coleslaw on the side, if desired.

Nutrition (per serving):

- Calories: 500
- Total Fat: 20g
- Saturated Fat: 6g
- Cholesterol: 100mg

- Sodium: 900mg
- Total Carbohydrate: 47g
- Dietary Fiber: 3g
- Sugars: 18g
- Protein: 32g

BBQ CHICKEN QUESADILLAS WITH PINEAPPLE SALSA

Cooking Time: 25 minutes
Servings: 4
Ingredients:
For the Quesadillas:

- 2 cups cooked chicken, shredded
- 1 cup barbecue sauce
- 8 medium flour tortillas
- 2 cups shredded cheese (cheddar or Mexican blend)

For the Pineapple Salsa:

- 1 cup diced pineapple
- 1/2 cup diced red bell pepper
- 1/4 cup diced red onion
- 1/4 cup chopped fresh cilantro
- One tablespoon of lime juice
- Salt and pepper to taste

Directions:

1. **Prepare the Chicken:** In a mixing bowl, combine shredded chicken and barbecue sauce until evenly coated.
2. **Make the Pineapple Salsa:** In another bowl, mix diced pineapple, red bell pepper, red onion, cilantro, lime juice, salt, and pepper. Set aside.

3. **Assemble the Quesadillas:** Lay out four tortillas on a clean surface. Divide the barbecue chicken mixture evenly among the tortillas, spreading it over one-half of each tortilla. Sprinkle shredded cheese over the chicken.

4. **Top with Another Tortilla:** Place the remaining four tortillas on the chicken and cheese mixture to form four quesadillas.

5. **Cook the Quesadillas:** Heat a large skillet or griddle over medium heat. Place one quesadilla onto the skillet and cook until the bottom tortilla is golden brown and crispy and the cheese is melted, about 2-3 minutes. Carefully flip the quesadilla and cook the other side until golden brown and the cheese is melted, about 2-3 minutes more. Repeat with remaining quesadillas.

6. **Serve:** Once cooked, transfer the quesadillas to a cutting board and let them cool for a minute before slicing them into wedges. Serve warm with pineapple salsa on the side.

Nutrition (per serving):

- Calories: 480
- Fat: 18g
- Saturated Fat: 9g
- Cholesterol: 85mg
- Sodium: 1100mg
- Carbohydrates: 49g
- Fiber: 3g
- Sugar: 19g
- Protein: 30g

GRILLED CHICKEN AND AVOCADO CAESAR WRAPS

Cooking Time: 20 minutes
Servings: 4
Ingredients:

- Four boneless, skinless chicken breasts
- Salt and pepper to taste

- Four large flour tortillas
- 2 cups romaine lettuce, chopped
- One ripe avocado, sliced
- ½ cup Caesar dressing
- ½ cup grated Parmesan cheese
- ½ cup croutons

Directions:

1. Preheat your grill to medium-high heat.
2. Season the chicken breasts with salt and pepper.
3. Grill the chicken for about 6-8 minutes per side until fully cooked through and no longer pink in the centre. Remove from the grill and let it rest for a few minutes before slicing.
4. Lay out the tortillas on a flat surface.
5. Divide the chopped romaine lettuce evenly among the tortillas, placing it in each centre.
6. Top the lettuce with slices of grilled chicken and avocado.
7. Drizzle each wrap with Caesar dressing.
8. Sprinkle-grated Parmesan cheese over the top of each wrap.
9. Add a handful of croutons to each wrap for added crunch.
10. Fold in the sides of the tortillas and roll them up tightly.
11. Serve immediately, or wrap each wrap in foil for an on-the-go meal.

Nutrition:

- CALORIES: 420 kcal
- PROTEIN: 32g
- CARBOHYDRATES: 23g
- FAT: 24g
- SATURATED FAT: 5g
- CHOLESTEROL: 80mg
- SODIUM: 760mg
- FIBER: 5g
- SUGAR: 3g

SMOKED BRISKET TACOS WITH CHIPOTLE CREMA

Cooking Time: 8 hours (including smoking time)
Servings: 4
Ingredients:

- 1 ½ lbs brisket, trimmed
- Eight small flour or corn tortillas
- One tablespoon of olive oil
- Salt and black pepper to taste

For the Dry Rub:
- Two tablespoons brown sugar
- 1 tablespoon smoked paprika
- One tablespoon chilli powder
- 1 tablespoon garlic powder
- One tablespoon of onion powder
- One teaspoon cumin
- 1 teaspoon black pepper
- 1 teaspoon salt

For the Chipotle Crema:
- ½ cup sour cream
- Two chipotle peppers in adobo sauce, minced
- One tablespoon of lime juice
- Salt to taste

For Serving (Optional):
- Chopped cilantro
- Diced onion
- Lime wedges

Directions:

1. **Prepare the Brisket:** In a small bowl, mix all the dry rub ingredients. Rub the dry rub all over the brisket, ensuring it's evenly coated. Wrap the brisket tightly in plastic wrap and refrigerate for at least 4 hours or overnight.

2. **Preheat the Smoker:** According to the manufacturer's instructions, preheat your smoker to 225°F (107°C). Add wood chips or chunks for a more flavorful smoke.

3. **Smoke the Brisket:** Place the seasoned brisket on the smoker grate and smoke for about 6-8 hours, or until the internal temperature reaches 195-205°F (90-96°C). Remove the brisket from the smoker and let it rest for 20-30 minutes before slicing.

4. **Prepare the Chipotle Crema:** In a small bowl, mix sour cream, minced chipotle peppers, lime juice, and salt. Adjust seasoning to taste. Refrigerate until ready to serve.

5. **Warm the Tortillas:** Heat a skillet over medium heat with a drizzle of olive oil. Warm each tortilla for about 30 seconds on each side until lightly golden and pliable. Wrap in a clean kitchen towel and keep warm.

6. **Assemble the Tacos:** Slice the smoked brisket thinly against the grain. Fill each tortilla with a generous portion of sliced brisket. Drizzle chipotle crema over the top. Serve with optional toppings such as chopped cilantro, diced onion, and lime wedges.

Nutrition (per serving):

- Calories: 450
- Total Fat: 20g
- Saturated Fat: 7g
- Cholesterol: 110mg
- Sodium: 820mg
- Total Carbohydrates: 31g
- Dietary Fiber: 3g
- Sugars: 4g
- Protein: 34g

WOOD-FIRED MARGHERITA PIZZA WITH FRESH BASIL

Cooking Time: 15 minutes
Servings: 4
Ingredients:

- 1 pound pizza dough at room temperature
- 1/2 cup marinara sauce
- 8 ounces fresh mozzarella cheese, thinly sliced
- 2-3 ripe tomatoes, thinly sliced
- Fresh basil leaves
- Olive oil
- Salt and pepper to taste

Directions:

1. Preheat your wood-fired oven to around 500-550°F (260-288°C). Ensure the oven is heated correctly and the wood has burned to embers.
2. Roll out the pizza dough on a floured surface to your desired thickness.
3. Transfer the dough to a pizza peel dusted with cornmeal or flour to prevent sticking.
4. Spread marinara sauce evenly over the dough, leaving a small border around the edges.
5. Arrange the slices of mozzarella cheese evenly over the sauce.
6. Place tomato slices on top of the cheese.
7. Drizzle olive oil over the pizza and season with salt and pepper to taste.
8. Carefully slide the pizza onto the preheated pizza stone in the wood-fired oven.

9. Bake for about 5-7 minutes until the crust is golden brown and the cheese is bubbly and melted.

10. Once cooked, remove the pizza from the oven using the pizza peel.

11. Tear fresh basil leaves and scatter them over the hot pizza.

12. Let the pizza cool for a minute before slicing.

13. Serve hot and enjoy your wood-fired Margherita pizza!

Nutrition:

- Serving Size: 1/4 of the pizza

- Calories: Approximately 300

- Total Fat: 12g

- Saturated Fat: 6g

- Cholesterol: 30mg

- Sodium: 680mg

- Total Carbohydrates: 32g

- Dietary Fiber: 2g

- Sugars: 4g

- Protein: 14g

BBQ PULLED CHICKEN SANDWICHES WITH TANGY SLAW

Cooking Time: 4 hours
Servings: 6
Ingredients:

- 2 lbs boneless, skinless chicken breasts

- 1 cup barbecue sauce

- 1/2 cup chicken broth

- Two tablespoons brown sugar

- One tablespoon of Worcestershire sauce

- One teaspoon of smoked paprika

- 1/2 teaspoon garlic powder
- 1/2 teaspoon onion powder
- Salt and pepper to taste
- Six hamburger buns

For the Tangy Slaw:

- 3 cups shredded cabbage
- 1/4 cup mayonnaise
- Two tablespoons of apple cider vinegar
- One tablespoon honey
- 1/2 teaspoon celery seed
- Salt and pepper to taste

Directions:

1. **Prepare the Chicken:** Place the chicken breasts in the slow cooker. In a bowl, mix barbecue sauce, chicken broth, brown sugar, Worcestershire sauce, smoked paprika, garlic powder, onion powder, salt, and pepper. Pour the mixture over the chicken.

2. **Cook:** Cover and cook on low heat for 4 hours until the chicken is tender and easily shredded with a fork.

3. **Shred the Chicken:** Once the chicken is cooked, remove it from the slow cooker and shred it using two forks. Return the shredded chicken to the slow cooker and stir it into the sauce.

4. **Prepare the Tangy Slaw:** In a separate bowl, combine shredded cabbage, mayonnaise, apple cider vinegar, honey, celery seed, salt, and pepper. Mix until well combined.

5. **Assemble the Sandwiches:** Toast the hamburger buns if desired. Place a generous portion of the BBQ-pulled chicken on the bottom half of each bun. Top with a scoop of tangy slaw. Place the top half of the bun on top.

6. **Serve:** If desired, the BBQ-pulled chicken sandwiches can be served with extra barbecue sauce and tangy slaw on the side.

TRAEGER GRILLED GREEK SALAD WITH LEMON VINAIGRETTE

Cooking Time: 20 minutes

 Servings: 4

Ingredients:

For the Salad:

- Two large tomatoes, cut into wedges
- One cucumber, sliced
- One red onion, thinly sliced
- One bell pepper, diced
- 1 cup Kalamata olives, pitted
- 1 cup feta cheese, crumbled
- 1/4 cup fresh parsley, chopped
- Salt and pepper to taste

For the Lemon Vinaigrette:

- 1/4 cup extra virgin olive oil
- Two tablespoons of fresh lemon juice
- One clove of garlic, minced
- One teaspoon dried oregano
- Salt and pepper to taste

Directions:

1. **Preheat the Traeger grill** to medium-high heat.

2. Combine the tomatoes, cucumber, red onion, bell pepper, Kalamata olives, and feta cheese in a large bowl.

3. To make the lemon vinaigrette, whisk together the olive oil, lemon juice, garlic, dried oregano, salt, and pepper in a separate small bowl.

4. Pour the lemon vinaigrette over the salad and toss gently to coat everything evenly.

5. Transfer the salad to a grill-safe tray or basket.

6. Place the tray or basket on the preheated Traeger grill and **grill** for about 10-12 minutes, or until the vegetables are slightly charred and tender, tossing occasionally to ensure even cooking.

7. Once grilled, remove the salad from the grill and transfer it back to the large bowl.

8. Sprinkle chopped parsley over the grilled salad and toss gently to combine.

9. Season with additional salt and pepper if needed.

10. Serve the Traeger Grilled Greek Salad with Lemon Vinaigrette immediately as a delicious and healthy side dish or light main course.

Nutrition: (PER SERVING)

- Calories: 280
- Fat: 22g
- Carbohydrates: 15g
- Fiber: 4g
- Protein: 7g

SMOKED TURKEY AND CRANBERRY PANINI

Cooking Time: 10 minutes
Servings: 2
Ingredients:

- Four slices of whole-wheat bread
- 6 oz smoked turkey breast, thinly sliced
- 1/2 cup cranberry sauce
- Four slices of Swiss cheese
- Two tablespoons butter softened

Directions:

1. Preheat a panini press or a skillet over medium heat.
2. Spread a tablespoon of cranberry sauce evenly on each slice of bread.
3. Layer the smoked turkey slices on two slices of bread.
4. Top the turkey with Swiss cheese slices.
5. Place the remaining slices of bread and cranberry side on the cheese.
6. Spread butter on the outsides of the sandwiches.
7. Place the sandwiches on the panini press or skillet and cook until the bread is golden brown and the cheese is melted about 4-5 minutes.
8. Remove from heat and let cool slightly before slicing diagonally.
9. Serve hot and enjoy your Smoked Turkey and Cranberry Panini!

Nutrition (per serving):

- Calories: 450
- Total Fat: 18g
- Saturated Fat: 10g
- Cholesterol: 85mg
- Sodium: 950mg
- Total Carbohydrates: 42g
- Dietary Fiber: 4g

- Sugars: 18g
- Protein: 28g

GRILLED SHRIMP TACOS WITH MANGO SALSA

Cooking Time: 20 minutes
Servings: 4
Ingredients:
For the Shrimp:

- 1 pound large shrimp, peeled and deveined
- Two tablespoons of olive oil
- One teaspoon of smoked paprika
- One teaspoon of garlic powder
- Salt and pepper to taste

For the Mango Salsa:

- Two ripe mangos, peeled and diced
- 1/4 cup red onion, finely chopped
- 1/4 cup fresh cilantro, chopped
- One jalapeño, seeded and minced
- Juice of 1 lime
- Salt to taste

For Serving:

- Eight small corn or flour tortillas
- One avocado, sliced
- 1/4 cup sour cream or Greek yoghurt
- Lime wedges for garnish
- Additional cilantro for garnish

Directions:

1. **Prepare the Shrimp:** In a bowl, combine the shrimp with olive oil, smoked paprika, garlic powder, salt, and pepper. Toss until the shrimp are evenly coated.

2. **Preheat the Grill:** Preheat your grill to medium-high heat.

3. **Grill the Shrimp:** Thread the shrimp onto skewers or place them directly on the grill grates. Grill for 2-3 minutes per side until the shrimp are pink and cooked through. Remove from the grill and set aside.

4. **Make the Mango Salsa:** In a bowl, combine the diced mango, red onion, cilantro, jalapeño, lime juice, and salt. Stir until well combined.

5. **Warm the Tortillas:** Heat the tortillas on the grill for about 30 seconds per side or until warmed through.

6. **Assemble the Tacos:** Divide the grilled shrimp among the warmed tortillas. Top with mango salsa, sliced avocado, and a sour cream or Greek yoghurt dollop.

7. **Garnish and Serve:** Garnish the tacos with additional cilantro and lime wedges. Serve immediately.

Nutrition: (PER SERVING)

- Calories: 350 kcal
- Total Fat: 12g
- Saturated Fat: 2g
- Cholesterol: 180mg
- Sodium: 450mg
- Total Carbohydrates: 40g
- Dietary Fiber: 6g
- Sugars: 12g
- Protein: 25g

BBQ PORK BELLY BAO BUNS

Cooking Time: 3 hours
Servings: 6
Ingredients:
For the Pork Belly:

- 1 lb pork belly, skin removed
- 3 cloves garlic, minced
- One tablespoon ginger, grated
- 1/4 cup soy sauce
- Two tablespoons of hoisin sauce
- 2 tablespoons honey
- One tablespoon of rice vinegar
- One tablespoon of sesame oil
- One teaspoon of Chinese five-spice powder

For the Bao Buns:

- 2 cups all-purpose flour
- One teaspoon of instant yeast
- One tablespoon sugar

- 1/2 cup warm water
- One tablespoon of vegetable oil
- Pinch of salt

For Garnish:

- Sliced green onions
- Fresh cilantro leaves
- Pickled cucumbers

Directions:

1. **Marinate the Pork Belly:** In a bowl, combine garlic, ginger, soy sauce, hoisin sauce, honey, rice vinegar, sesame oil, and Chinese five-spice powder. Place the pork belly in a shallow dish and pour the marinade over it. Cover and refrigerate for at least 2 hours or overnight.

2. **Cook the Pork Belly:** Preheat the oven to 325°F (160°C). Remove the pork belly from the marinade and place it in a baking dish. Reserve the marinade. Roast the pork belly in the oven for 2-2.5 hours until tender and caramelized. Baste with the reserved marinade occasionally.

3. **Make the Bao Buns:** In a large mixing bowl, combine flour, instant yeast, sugar, and salt. Gradually add warm water while mixing until a dough forms. Knead the dough on a floured surface for about 5-7 minutes until it becomes smooth and elastic. Place the dough in a greased bowl, cover it with a clean kitchen towel, and let it rest in a warm place for 1 hour or until it doubles in size.

4. **Form the Bao Buns:** After the dough has risen, punch it down and divide it into 6 equal portions. Roll each portion into a ball and flatten it into an oval shape using a rolling pin. Brush the surface of each oval with vegetable oil. Fold each oval in half, then place a square piece of parchment paper underneath each bun. Let the buns rest for 15-20 minutes.

5. **Steam the Bao Buns:** In a steamer, bring water to a boil. Place the parchment paper squares with the buns in the steamer basket, leaving enough space between them. Steam the buns for 10-12 minutes until puffed and cooked through.

6. **Assemble the Bao Buns:** Slice the cooked pork belly into thin pieces. Open each steamed bun and fill it with slices of pork belly. Garnish with sliced green onions, cilantro leaves, and pickled cucumbers.

Nutrition: (PER SERVING)

- Calories: 420
- Total Fat: 22g
- Saturated Fat: 8g
- Cholesterol: 60mg
- Sodium: 780mg
- Total Carbohydrates: 36g

- Dietary Fiber: 2g
- Sugars: 7g
- Protein: 18g

WOOD-FIRED VEGETABLE FLATBREAD WITH BALSAMIC GLAZE

Cooking Time: 20 minutes
Servings: 4
Ingredients:

- 1 pound pizza dough, store-bought or homemade
- One medium zucchini, thinly sliced
- One medium yellow squash, thinly sliced
- One red bell pepper, thinly sliced
- One yellow bell pepper, thinly sliced
- One red onion, thinly sliced
- Two tablespoons of olive oil
- Salt and pepper to taste
- 1/4 cup balsamic glaze
- Fresh basil leaves for garnish

Directions:

1. Preheat your wood-fired oven to about 500°F (260°C). If you don't have a wood-fired oven, you can use a regular oven preheated to the highest temperature.
2. While the oven is heating, prepare the vegetables. In a large bowl, toss the zucchini, yellow squash, red bell pepper, yellow bell pepper, and red onion with olive oil, salt, and pepper until evenly coated.
3. Roll out the pizza dough on a floured surface into a rectangular, about 1/4 inch thick.
4. Carefully transfer the rolled-out dough onto a floured pizza peel or parchment paper.
5. Arrange the seasoned vegetables evenly over the dough, leaving a small border around the edges.
6. Slide the flatbread onto the oven's preheated pizza stone or baking sheet.
7. Bake for about 10-12 minutes until the crust is golden brown and the vegetables are tender and slightly charred.
8. Once cooked, remove the flatbread from the oven and drizzle with balsamic glaze.
9. Garnish with fresh basil leaves before serving.

TRAEGER SMOKED BEEF FAJITAS WITH GUACAMOLE

Cooking Time: 2 hours
 Servings: 4
Ingredients:

- 1 pound flank steak
- One red bell pepper, sliced
- One yellow bell pepper, sliced
- One green bell pepper, sliced
- One large onion, sliced
- Two cloves garlic, minced
- Two tablespoons of olive oil
- Two teaspoons chilli powder
- One teaspoon of ground cumin
- One teaspoon paprika
- Salt and pepper to taste
- Eight flour tortillas
- Fresh cilantro leaves for garnish

For the Guacamole:

- 2 ripe avocados, peeled and pitted
- One small red onion, finely chopped
- One tomato, diced
- One jalapeño, seeded and finely chopped
- Juice of 1 lime
- Salt and pepper to taste

Directions:

1. **Preheat your Traeger smoker to 225°F (107°C).**
2. Mix the chilli powder, cumin, paprika, minced garlic, salt, and pepper in a small bowl.
3. Rub the spice mixture evenly over the flank steak.
4. Place the seasoned flank steak directly on the smoker grate and smoke for 1 hour.
5. After 1 hour, increase the temperature of the smoker to 375°F (190°C).
6. Toss the sliced bell peppers and onions with olive oil, salt, and pepper in a large bowl.
7. Spread the seasoned vegetables on a grill tray or aluminium foil and place them on the smoker alongside the steak.
8. Continue smoking the steak and vegetables for an additional 30-45 minutes, or until the steak reaches your desired level of doneness and the vegetables are tender and slightly charred.

9. Remove the steak and vegetables from the smoker and let the steak rest for 10 minutes before slicing thinly against the grain.

10. While the steak is resting, prepare the guacamole. In a medium bowl, mash the avocados with a fork until smooth.

11. Stir in the chopped red onion, diced tomato, jalapeño, lime juice, salt, and pepper until well combined.

12. Warm the flour tortillas on the smoker for a few minutes, then assemble the fajitas by filling each tortilla with slices of smoked flank steak and smoked vegetables.

13. Serve the Traeger Smoked Beef Fajitas with Guacamole, garnished with fresh cilantro leaves.

Nutrition (per serving):

Calories: 480

Total Fat: 23g

- Saturated Fat: 5g
- Cholesterol: 55mg
- Sodium: 570mg
- Total Carbohydrates: 42g
- Dietary Fiber: 9g
- Sugars: 5g
- Protein: 28g

GRILLED CHICKEN CAESAR SALAD WRAPS

Cooking Time: 20 minutes

Servings: 4

Ingredients:

- Four boneless, skinless chicken breasts
- Salt and pepper to taste
- Four large tortilla wraps
- 4 cups romaine lettuce, chopped
- 1 cup cherry tomatoes, halved
- 1/2 cup grated Parmesan cheese
- 1/2 cup Caesar salad dressing
- Olive oil for grilling

Directions:

1. Preheat your grill to medium-high heat.

2. Season chicken breasts with salt and pepper.

3. Drizzle olive oil over the chicken breasts and rub to coat.

4. Grill chicken breasts for 6-7 minutes per side or until fully cooked (internal temperature reaches 165°F or 75°C). Remove from grill and let rest for a few minutes.

5. Slice grilled chicken into strips.

6. Lay out tortilla wraps on a clean surface.

7. Divide chopped romaine lettuce evenly among the wraps.

8. Add sliced grilled chicken on top of the lettuce.

9. Sprinkle cherry tomatoes and grated Parmesan cheese over the chicken.

10. Drizzle Caesar salad dressing over the fillings.

11. Carefully fold in the sides of the tortilla wraps, then roll them up tightly, enclosing the fillings.

12. Slice each wrap in half diagonally.

13. Serve immediately and enjoy!

Nutrition (per serving):

- Calories: 480
- Total Fat: 25g
- Saturated Fat: 6g
- Cholesterol: 110mg
- Sodium: 920mg
- Total Carbohydrate: 26g
- Dietary Fiber: 3g
- Sugars: 4g
- Protein: 38g

SMOKED SAUSAGE AND PEPPER HOAGIES

Cooking Time: 30 minutes
Servings: 4
Ingredients:

- One package (14 ounces) of smoked sausage, sliced
- Two bell peppers (red, yellow, or green), thinly sliced
- One onion, thinly sliced
- Two cloves garlic, minced
- One tablespoon of olive oil
- Salt and pepper to taste

- Four hoagie rolls
- 4 slices provolone cheese
- Optional toppings: marinara sauce, mustard, mayonnaise, pickles

Directions:

1. Heat olive oil in a large skillet over medium heat. Add sliced smoked sausage and cook until lightly browned about 5 minutes.

2. Add sliced bell peppers, onions, and minced garlic to the skillet. Cook, stirring occasionally, until the vegetables are tender, about 8-10 minutes. Season with salt and pepper to taste.

3. While the sausage and peppers are cooking, preheat your oven to 350°F (175°C). Slice the hoagie rolls lengthwise, leaving one side intact, and open them up like a book.

4. Place the opened hoagie rolls on a baking sheet lined with parchment paper. On one side of each hoagie roll, place a slice of provolone cheese.

5. Once the sausage and peppers are cooked, evenly distribute them among the hoagie rolls on top of the cheese.

6. Add optional toppings such as marinara sauce, mustard, mayonnaise, or pickles if desired.

7. Close the hoagie rolls and wrap them loosely in foil. Place them in the oven and bake for 5-7 minutes until the cheese is melted and the hoagie rolls are heated.

8. Remove from the oven, unwrap the subs, and serve hot.

Nutrition: NUTRITION VALUES MAY VARY DEPENDING ON SPECIFIC INGREDIENTS AND SERVING SIZES.

- Calories: Approximately 450 per serving
- Total Fat: 25g
- Saturated Fat: 9g
- Cholesterol: 55mg
- Sodium: 1100mg
- Total Carbohydrates: 36g
- Dietary Fiber: 3g
- Sugars: 6g
- Protein: 18g

BBQ PORK RIB SANDWICHES WITH SPICY PICKLES

Cooking Time: 3 hours 30 minutes
Servings: 4
Ingredients:

- One rack of pork ribs (about 2 pounds)

- Salt and black pepper to taste
- 1 cup BBQ sauce
- Four sandwich buns
- 1 cup spicy pickles, thinly sliced
- 1/2 cup coleslaw (optional)

Directions:

1. **Preheat the oven to 300°F (150°C).**

2. **Prepare the ribs:** Remove the membrane from the back of the ribs. Season the ribs generously with salt and black pepper.

3. **Slow-cook the ribs:** Place the ribs on a baking sheet lined with aluminum foil. Cover tightly with another sheet of foil and roast in the preheated oven for 2.5 to 3 hours, or until the meat is tender and pulls away from the bones.

4. **Prepare the BBQ sauce:** While the ribs are cooking, heat the BBQ sauce in a small saucepan over low heat, stirring occasionally.

5. **Finish the ribs:** Once the ribs are done, remove them from the oven and increase the oven temperature to 400°F (200°C). Brush the ribs generously with the warmed BBQ sauce.

6. **Broil the ribs:** Return the ribs to the oven and broil for 5-10 minutes or until the sauce is caramelized and sticky.

7. **Assemble the sandwiches:** Slice the ribs into individual portions. Place a portion of ribs on each sandwich bun. Top with sliced spicy pickles and coleslaw if desired. Serve immediately.

Nutrition:
(PER SERVING)

- Calories: 600
- Total Fat: 26g
- Saturated Fat: 8g
- Cholesterol: 120mg
- Sodium: 1200mg
- Total Carbohydrates: 52g
- Dietary Fiber: 2g
- Sugars: 22g
- Protein: 40g

TRAEGER GRILLED CAPRESE SANDWICHES WITH PESTO

Cooking Time: 15 minutes
Servings: 4

Ingredients:

- Eight slices of rustic bread
- Two large tomatoes, thinly sliced
- 1 pound fresh mozzarella cheese, sliced
- 1 cup fresh basil leaves
- ½ cup pine nuts
- Two cloves garlic
- ½ cup grated Parmesan cheese
- ½ cup extra-virgin olive oil
- Salt and pepper to taste
- Balsamic glaze (optional)

Directions:

1. **Prepare the Pesto:** In a food processor, combine basil leaves, pine nuts, garlic, Parmesan cheese, and olive oil. Pulse until smooth. Season with salt and pepper to taste. Set aside.

2. **Preheat the Traeger Grill:** Preheat your Traeger Grill to 350°F (175°C) according to manufacturer instructions.

3. **Assemble the Sandwiches:** Take four slices of bread and spread a generous amount of pesto on each slice. Top with slices of tomato and mozzarella cheese. Place another slice of bread on top to form sandwiches.

4. **Grill the Sandwiches:** Place the assembled sandwiches directly on the grill grate. Close the lid and grill for about 5-7 minutes on each side, or until the bread is toasted and the cheese is melted.

5. **Serve:** Once the sandwiches are grilled to perfection, remove them and let them cool for a minute or two. Optionally, drizzle with balsamic glaze for extra flavour. Serve warm and enjoy!

Nutrition:

- NUTRITIONAL INFORMATION PER SERVING (1 SANDWICH):
    - Calories: 590
    - Total Fat: 40g
    - Saturated Fat: 13g
    - Cholesterol: 65mg
    - Sodium: 680mg
    - Total Carbohydrates: 34g
    - Dietary Fiber: 4g
    - Sugars: 5g
    - Protein: 25g

SMOKED BBQ RIBS WITH HOMEMADE SAUCE

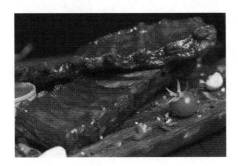

Cooking Time: 4 hours
Servings: 4-6
Ingredients:

- Two racks of pork baby back ribs (about 2 1/2 to 3 pounds each)
- 1 tablespoon paprika
- One tablespoon brown sugar
- One tablespoon garlic powder
- One tablespoon onion powder
- 1 teaspoon cumin
- One teaspoon chilli powder
- Salt and pepper to taste

For the Homemade BBQ Sauce:

- 1 cup ketchup
- 1/2 cup apple cider vinegar
- 1/4 cup brown sugar
- Two tablespoons Worcestershire sauce
- One tablespoon Dijon mustard
- One teaspoon smoked paprika
- One teaspoon garlic powder
- Salt and pepper to taste

Directions:

1. **Prepare the Ribs:** Remove the membrane from the back of the ribs. Mix paprika, brown sugar, garlic powder, onion powder, cumin, chilli powder, salt, and pepper in a small bowl. Rub this spice mixture evenly over the ribs. Let them sit at room temperature for about 30 minutes while you prepare the smoker.

2. **Preheat the Smoker:** Preheat your smoker to 225°F (107°C), using your choice of wood chips for smoking.

3. **Smoke the Ribs:** Place the ribs directly on the grill grates once the smoker is ready. Close the lid and smoke the ribs for about 3 to 4 hours or until the meat is tender and pulls away from the bone.

4. **Make the BBQ Sauce:** While the ribs are smoking, prepare the BBQ sauce. Combine ketchup, apple cider vinegar, brown sugar, Worcestershire sauce, Dijon mustard, smoked paprika, garlic powder, salt, and pepper in a saucepan. Bring the mixture to a simmer over medium heat, then reduce the heat to low and let it simmer for about 15-20 minutes, stirring occasionally, until the sauce thickens slightly.

5. **Finish the Ribs:** During the last 30 minutes of smoking, brush the ribs generously with the homemade BBQ sauce and coat them evenly. Close the lid and continue smoking until the sauce caramelises and the ribs tender.

6. **Serve:** Once the ribs are done, remove them from the smoker and rest for a few minutes. Cut between the bones to separate the ribs, then serve them hot with extra BBQ sauce on the side.

Nutrition: (per serving, assuming six servings)

- Calories: 580
- Total Fat: 36g
- Saturated Fat: 13g
- Cholesterol: 150mg
- Sodium: 860mg
- Total Carbohydrates: 21g
- Dietary Fiber: 1g
- Sugars: 16g
- Protein: 43g

TRAEGER GRILLED TRI-TIP STEAK WITH GARLIC BUTTER

Cooking Time: 1 hour 30 minutes
Servings: 4-6
Ingredients:

- One tri-tip steak (about 2-3 pounds)
- Four cloves garlic, minced
- 1/2 cup unsalted butter, softened
- Two tablespoons olive oil
- Two teaspoons salt
- One teaspoon black pepper
- One teaspoon smoked paprika
- One teaspoon dried thyme
- One teaspoon dried rosemary

Directions:

1. **Prepare the Garlic Butter:** Combine minced garlic and softened butter in a small bowl. Mix well until fully incorporated. Set aside.

2. **Preheat the Traeger Grill:** Preheat your Traeger grill to 250°F (120°C) using hickory or mesquite wood pellets for added flavour.

3. **Season the Tri-Tip Steak:** Rub the Tri-Tip steak with olive oil, then season it generously with salt, black pepper, smoked paprika, dried thyme, and dried rosemary. Ensure the seasoning is evenly distributed on all sides of the steak.

4. **Grill the Tri-Tip Steak:** Place the seasoned tri-tip steak directly on the grill grate and close the lid. Let it cook for about 45 minutes to 1 hour or until the internal temperature reaches 125°F (52°C) for medium-rare doneness.

5. **Apply Garlic Butter:** Once the tri-tip steak reaches the desired internal temperature, remove it from the grill and rest for 10 minutes. Slice the steak against the grain into thin slices. Spread the prepared garlic butter over the sliced steak while still warm, allowing it to melt and infuse the meat with flavour.

6. **Serve:** Arrange the sliced tri-tip steak on a serving platter and drizzle any remaining garlic butter over the top. Serve hot and enjoy the succulent Traeger grilled tri-tip steak with garlic butter.

Nutrition:
(NUTRITIONAL VALUES ARE APPROXIMATE AND MAY VARY DEPENDING ON PORTION SIZES AND INGREDIENTS USED.)

- **Calories:** 400 kcal
- **Total Fat:** 32g
- **Saturated Fat:** 14g
- **Cholesterol:** 120mg
- **Sodium:** 1170mg
- **Total Carbohydrates:** 2g
- **Dietary Fiber:** 0g
- **Sugars:** 0g
- **Protein:** 26g

WOOD-FIRED HONEY MUSTARD GLAZED SALMON

Cooking Time: 20 minutes
Servings: 4
Ingredients:

- Four salmon fillets (about 6 ounces each)
- 1/4 cup honey
- Three tablespoons Dijon mustard
- Two tablespoons soy sauce
- Two cloves garlic, minced
- One tablespoon olive oil
- Salt and pepper to taste
- Lemon wedges for serving

- Fresh parsley, chopped (optional, for garnish)

Directions:

1. Preheat your wood-fired grill to medium-high heat, around 375-400°F (190-200°C).

2. In a small bowl, whisk together honey, Dijon mustard, soy sauce, minced garlic, olive oil, salt, and pepper until well combined.

3. Place the salmon fillets on a large plate or tray and generously brush both sides with the honey mustard mixture, reserving some for basting while grilling.

4. Once the grill is preheated, lightly oil the grates to prevent sticking. Place the salmon fillets directly onto the grill, skin-side down.

5. Close the grill lid and cook the salmon for about 4-5 minutes per side, or until the fish flakes easily with a fork and is cooked to your desired level of doneness.

6. While grilling, occasionally baste the salmon with the remaining honey mustard glaze to add flavour and keep the fish moist.

7. Once the salmon is cooked through, carefully remove it from the grill using a spatula and transfer it to a serving platter.

8. Garnish the wood-fired honey mustard glazed salmon with fresh chopped parsley, and serve hot with lemon wedges on the side.

Nutrition: (NUTRITIONAL VALUES ARE APPROXIMATE AND MAY VARY DEPENDING ON SPECIFIC INGREDIENTS USED)

- Calories: 320 kcal
- Protein: 34g
- Fat: 16g
- Carbohydrates: 12g
- Fibre: 0.5g
- Sugar: 11g
- Sodium: 650mg

GRILLED BBQ CHICKEN THIGHS WITH ALABAMA WHITE SAUCE

Cooking Time: 25 minutes
Servings: 4
Ingredients:

- Eight bone-in, skin-on chicken thighs
- Salt and pepper to taste
- 1 cup BBQ sauce (your favourite brand)
- 1 cup mayonnaise
- Two tablespoons apple cider vinegar

- One tablespoon lemon juice
- One tablespoon honey
- 1 teaspoon horseradish
- One teaspoon Dijon mustard
- One teaspoon garlic powder
- One teaspoon onion powder
- 1/2 teaspoon smoked paprika
- 1/4 teaspoon cayenne pepper (optional)
- Chopped fresh parsley or chives for garnish (optional)

Directions:

1. **Preheat the Grill:** Preheat your grill to medium-high heat, around 375-400°F (190-200°C).

2. **Season the Chicken:** Pat the chicken thighs dry with paper towels and season generously with salt and pepper.

3. **Make the BBQ Sauce:** In a small bowl, mix the BBQ sauce, apple cider vinegar, honey, garlic powder, onion powder, smoked paprika, and cayenne pepper (if using). Set aside.

4. **Grill the Chicken:** Place the thighs skin-side down on the preheated grill. Grill for 6-8 minutes per side until the internal temperature reaches 165°F (74°C) and the juices run clear. During the last few minutes of grilling, brush the chicken thighs with the prepared BBQ sauce, flipping occasionally to prevent burning.

5. **Make the Alabama White Sauce:** While the chicken is grilling, whisk the mayonnaise, lemon juice, horseradish, and Dijon mustard in another bowl until well combined—season with salt and pepper to taste.

6. **Serve:** Once the chicken is cooked and nicely charred, remove it from the grill and rest for a few minutes. Serve the grilled BBQ chicken thighs with the Alabama white sauce on the side for dipping, or drizzle the sauce over the chicken. Garnish with chopped fresh parsley or chives if desired.

Nutrition: NOTE: NUTRITIONAL VALUES MAY VARY DEPENDING ON THE INGREDIENTS AND BRANDS USED.

- Calories: 450 kcal
- Total Fat: 28g
    - Saturated Fat: 6g
    - Trans Fat: 0g
- Cholesterol: 180mg
- Sodium: 950mg
- Total Carbohydrate: 18g
    - Dietary Fiber: 1g
    - Sugars: 15g

- Protein: 34g

SMOKED BEEF BRISKET WITH COFFEE RUB

Cooking Time: 10-12 hours
Servings: 8-10
Ingredients:

- 1 (8-10 pound) beef brisket, trimmed of excess fat
- 1/4 cup finely ground coffee
- Two tablespoons brown sugar
- Two tablespoons paprika
- One tablespoon kosher salt
- 1 tablespoon black pepper
- One tablespoon garlic powder
- One tablespoon onion powder
- 1 teaspoon cayenne pepper
- Two tablespoons olive oil
- Wood chips (such as hickory or oak) soaked in water for at least 30 minutes

Directions:

1. In a small bowl, mix the finely ground coffee, brown sugar, paprika, kosher salt, black pepper, garlic powder, onion powder, and cayenne pepper to make the coffee rub.

2. Pat the brisket dry with paper towels and rub it all over with olive oil. Then, coat the brisket with the coffee rub, covering all sides evenly. Let the brisket sit at room temperature for about 30 minutes to allow the flavours to penetrate.

3. Meanwhile, prepare your smoker according to manufacturer instructions and preheat it to 225°F (107°C). Add soaked wood chips to the smoker box.

4. Once the smoker is ready, place the brisket directly on the grill grate, fat side up. Close the lid and smoke the brisket for 10-12 hours, or until the internal temperature reaches 195-205°F (90-96°C) and the meat is tender.

5. Occasionally check the smoker's temperature and add more soaked wood chips to maintain a steady smoke.

6. Once done, carefully remove the brisket from the smoker and transfer it to a cutting board. Tent the brisket loosely with foil and let it rest for about 30 minutes to allow the juices to redistribute.

7. Slice the brisket against the grain into thin slices and serve hot. Enjoy your delicious Smoked Beef Brisket with Coffee Rub!

Nutrition: (per serving, assuming ten servings)

- Calories: 450
- Total Fat: 26g
- Saturated Fat: 9g
- Cholesterol: 150mg
- Sodium: 700mg
- Total Carbohydrates: 3g
- Dietary Fiber: 1g
- Sugars: 2g
- Protein: 48g

BBQ PULLED PORK MAC AND CHEESE

Cooking Time: 2 hours
Servings: 6-8
Ingredients:
- 1 pound elbow macaroni
- 2 cups shredded BBQ pulled pork
- 2 cups shredded cheddar cheese
- 1 cup shredded mozzarella cheese
- 1/2 cup BBQ sauce
- 1/4 cup butter
- 1/4 cup all-purpose flour
- 2 cups milk
- Salt and pepper to taste
- 1/2 cup breadcrumbs (optional)

- Chopped fresh parsley for garnish (optional)

Directions:

1. Preheat your oven to 350°F (175°C). Grease a 9x13-inch baking dish.

2. Cook the elbow macaroni according to package instructions until al dente. Drain and set aside.

3. In a large skillet, melt the butter over medium heat. Once melted, whisk in the flour to create a roux. Cook for 1-2 minutes, stirring constantly, until the mixture is golden brown.

4. Gradually pour in the milk while whisking continuously to prevent lumps from forming. Cook until the mixture thickens, about 3-5 minutes.

5. Stir in the shredded cheddar and mozzarella cheese until melted and smooth—season with salt and pepper to taste.

6. Add the cooked macaroni and shredded BBQ pulled pork to the cheese sauce. Stir until well combined.

7. Pour half of the mac and cheese mixture into the prepared baking dish. Drizzle half of the BBQ sauce over the top. Repeat with the remaining mac and cheese and BBQ sauce.

8. Sprinkle breadcrumbs evenly over the mac and cheese for a crunchy topping.

9. Bake in the preheated oven for 25-30 minutes or until the cheese is bubbly and golden brown on top.

10. Remove the dish from the oven and let it cool for a few minutes before serving. If desired, garnish with chopped fresh parsley.

Nutrition:

NUTRITIONAL INFORMATION WILL VARY DEPENDING ON SPECIFIC BRANDS OF INGREDIENTS AND SERVING SIZES. HOWEVER, HERE'S A ROUGH ESTIMATE PER SERVING BASED ON THE RECIPE AS DESCRIBED:

- Calories: 550

- Total Fat: 25g

- Saturated Fat: 14g

- Cholesterol: 110mg

- Sodium: 800mg

- Total Carbohydrates: 50g

- Dietary Fiber: 2g

- Sugars: 12g

- Protein: 30g

GRILLED HONEY GARLIC SHRIMP SKEWERS

Cooking Time: 15 minutes
Servings: 4
Ingredients:

- 1 pound large shrimp, peeled and deveined
- Two tablespoons honey
- 3 cloves garlic, minced
- Two tablespoons soy sauce
- 1 tablespoon olive oil
- One tablespoon lemon juice
- One teaspoon paprika
- Salt and pepper to taste
- Wooden skewers, soaked in water for 30 minutes

Directions:

1. Whisk together honey, minced garlic, soy sauce, olive oil, lemon juice, paprika, salt, and pepper in a small bowl.

2. Place the shrimp in a resealable plastic bag and pour the marinade over them. Seal the bag and marinate in the refrigerator for at least 30 minutes or up to 2 hours.

3. Preheat the grill to medium-high heat.

4. Thread the marinated shrimp onto the soaked wooden skewers, leaving a little space between each shrimp.

5. Grill the shrimp skewers on each side for 2-3 minutes or until they are opaque and grill marks appear.

6. Remove the skewers from the grill and serve hot.

Nutrition (per serving):

- Calories: 180
- Total Fat: 5g
- Saturated Fat: 1g
- Cholesterol: 215mg

- Sodium: 640mg
- Total Carbohydrate: 10g
- Dietary Fiber: 0.5g
- Sugars: 8g
- Protein: 24g

TRAEGER SMOKED MEATLOAF WITH BROWN SUGAR GLAZE

Cooking Time: 2 hours
Servings: 6-8
Ingredients:
For the Meatloaf:

- 2 lbs ground beef (preferably 80/20)
- 1 cup breadcrumbs
- Two eggs, beaten
- 1 onion, finely chopped
- Two cloves garlic, minced
- 1/4 cup ketchup
- Two tablespoons Worcestershire sauce
- One teaspoon salt
- 1/2 teaspoon black pepper
- 1/2 teaspoon smoked paprika
- 1/4 teaspoon dried thyme
- 1/4 teaspoon dried oregano
- 1/4 teaspoon dried parsley

For the Glaze:

- 1/2 cup ketchup
- 1/4 cup brown sugar
- One tablespoon apple cider vinegar
- One teaspoon Dijon mustard

Directions:

1. **Prepare the Meatloaf Mixture:**
   - In a large mixing bowl, combine ground beef, breadcrumbs, beaten eggs, chopped onion, minced garlic, ketchup, Worcestershire sauce, salt, black pepper, smoked paprika, dried thyme, dried oregano, and dried parsley. Mix until well combined.

1. **Form the Meatloaf:**

- Shape the meat mixture into a loaf shape and place it on aluminium foil. Mold and shape it until it resembles a loaf, ensuring it's compacted but not overly dense.

1. **Preheat the Traeger Smoker:**
   - Preheat your Traeger smoker to 225°F (107°C) according to the manufacturer's instructions.

1. **Smoke the Meatloaf:**
   - Place the meatloaf on the smoker grate and close the lid. Let it smoke for about 1.5 to 2 hours or until the internal temperature reaches 160°F (71°C).

1. **Prepare the Glaze:**
   - While the meatloaf is smoking, prepare the glaze. Combine ketchup, brown sugar, apple cider vinegar, and Dijon mustard in a small saucepan. Cook over medium heat, stirring constantly, until the brown sugar is completely dissolved. Remove from heat.

1. **Apply the Glaze:**
   - About 15 minutes before the meatloaf is done, brush the glaze generously over the top of the meatloaf.

1. **Finish Smoking:**
   - Close the lid of the Traeger smoker and let the meatloaf smoke for another 15 minutes, allowing the glaze to caramelize.

1. **Serve:**
   - Once the meatloaf is done smoking and has reached an internal temperature of 160°F (71°C), carefully remove it. Let it rest for a few minutes before slicing. Serve warm.

Nutrition:

- NOTE: NUTRITION INFORMATION IS APPROXIMATE AND MAY VARY BASED ON SPECIFIC INGREDIENTS.
- Serving Size: 1 slice (assuming eight servings)
- Calories: 350
- Total Fat: 15g
- Saturated Fat: 6g
- Cholesterol: 125mg
- Sodium: 750mg
- Total Carbohydrate: 22g
- Dietary Fiber: 1g
- Sugars: 11g
- Protein: 28g

WOOD-FIRED BARBECUE CHICKEN PIZZA WITH RED ONIONS

Cooking Time: 20 minutes

Servings: 4

Ingredients:

- 1 pound pizza dough at room temperature
- 1 cup barbecue sauce
- 2 cups cooked chicken breast, shredded
- 1 cup red onion, thinly sliced
- 2 cups shredded mozzarella cheese
- Fresh cilantro leaves for garnish (optional)
- Olive oil for brushing

Directions:

1. Preheat your wood-fired pizza oven to 500°F (260°C).
2. Roll out the pizza dough on a floured surface to your desired thickness.
3. Transfer the dough to a pizza peel or a lightly floured pizza pan.
4. Brush the surface of the dough with olive oil.
5. Spread the barbecue sauce evenly over the dough, leaving a small border around the edges.
6. Sprinkle the shredded chicken evenly over the barbecue sauce.
7. Scatter the sliced red onions over the chicken.
8. Top with shredded mozzarella cheese.
9. Carefully slide the pizza onto the preheated pizza stone in the oven.
10. Bake for about 8-10 minutes until the crust is golden brown and the cheese is bubbly and melted.
11. Once done, remove the pizza from the oven and let it cool for a minute or two.
12. Garnish with fresh cilantro leaves if desired.
13. Slice and serve hot.

Nutrition:

- Serving Size: 1 slice (assuming eight slices per pizza)
- Calories: Approximately 380
- Total Fat: 12g
- Saturated Fat: 5g
- Cholesterol: 60mg
- Sodium: 950mg

- Total Carbohydrates: 44g
- Dietary Fiber: 2g
- Sugars: 14g
- Protein: 25g

SMOKED SAUSAGE AND POTATO FOIL PACKETS

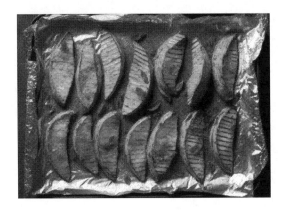

Cooking Time: 30 minutes
Servings: 4
Ingredients:

- Four smoked sausages, sliced into rounds
- Four medium potatoes, thinly sliced
- One onion, thinly sliced
- One bell pepper, thinly sliced
- Two cloves garlic, minced
- Two tablespoons olive oil
- Salt and pepper to taste
- One teaspoon paprika
- One teaspoon dried thyme
- 1/2 teaspoon garlic powder
- 1/2 teaspoon onion powder
- Chopped fresh parsley for garnish (optional)

Directions:

1. Preheat your oven to 400°F (200°C).
2. Tear off four large pieces of heavy-duty aluminium foil, about 12 inches in length each.

3. Combine the sliced smoked sausage, potatoes, onion, bell pepper, and minced garlic in a large bowl.

4. Drizzle olive oil over the mixture and toss to coat evenly.

5. Season with salt, pepper, paprika, dried thyme, garlic powder, and onion powder. Toss again until everything is well coated with the seasonings.

6. Divide the mixture evenly among the aluminium foil pieces, placing it in the centre of each foil.

7. Fold the sides of the foil over the sausage and potato mixture, sealing tightly to form packets.

8. Place the foil packets on a baking sheet and bake in the oven for 25-30 minutes or until the potatoes are tender.

9. Carefully open the foil packets (watch out for steam) and transfer the contents to serving plates.

10. Garnish with chopped fresh parsley if desired, and serve hot.

Nutrition: (PER SERVING)

Calories: 375 kcal

Total Fat: 22g

- Saturated Fat: 6g
- Cholesterol: 40mg
- Sodium: 720mg
- Total Carbohydrates: 30g
- Dietary Fiber: 4g
- Sugars: 3g
- Protein: 15g

GRILLED TERIYAKI PORK CHOPS WITH PINEAPPLE SALSA

Cooking Time: 25 minutes
Servings: 4
Ingredients:
For the Teriyaki Pork Chops:

- Four pork chops (about 1 inch thick)
- ½ cup soy sauce
- ¼ cup brown sugar
- 2 cloves garlic, minced
- One teaspoon ginger, minced
- Two tablespoons rice vinegar
- 1 tablespoon sesame oil
- One tablespoon cornstarch
- Salt and pepper to taste

For the Pineapple Salsa:

- 1 cup fresh pineapple, diced
- ½ red bell pepper, diced
- 1 jalapeño pepper, seeded and minced
- ¼ cup red onion, finely chopped
- Two tablespoons fresh cilantro, chopped
- Juice of 1 lime
- Salt to taste

Directions:

1. **Marinate the Pork Chops:** In a bowl, whisk together soy sauce, brown sugar, minced garlic, minced ginger, rice vinegar, sesame oil, cornstarch, salt, and pepper. Place the pork chops in a shallow dish or a resealable plastic bag and pour the marinade over them. Make sure the pork chops are well coated—Marinate in the refrigerator for at least 30 minutes or up to 4 hours.

2. **Prepare the Pineapple Salsa:** In another bowl, combine diced pineapple, red bell pepper, minced jalapeño pepper, chopped red onion, chopped cilantro, lime juice, and salt. Mix well and refrigerate until ready to serve.

3. **Preheat the Grill:** Preheat your grill to medium-high heat (about 375°F to 400°F).

4. **Grill the Pork Chops:** Remove the pork chops from the marinade and discard any excess marinade. Place the pork chops on the preheated grill and cook for about 5-6 minutes per side until the internal temperature reaches 145°F, turning once halfway through cooking. Cooking time may vary depending on the thickness of the pork chops.

5. **Serve:** Once the pork chops are cooked, remove them from the grill and rest for a few minutes. Serve the grilled teriyaki pork chops hot, topped with pineapple salsa.

Nutrition:

(NUTRITIONAL VALUES ARE APPROXIMATE AND MAY VARY DEPENDING ON THE INGREDIENTS USED.)

- **Calories:** 320 kcal

- **Protein:** 28g
- **Fat:** 14g
- **Carbohydrates:** 20g
- **Fiber:** 2g
- **Sugar:** 14g
- **Sodium:** 1240mg

BBQ STUFFED BELL PEPPERS WITH GROUND BEEF AND RICE

Cooking Time: 1 hour 15 minutes
Servings: 4
Ingredients:

- Four large bell peppers (any colour)
- 1 pound ground beef
- 1 cup cooked rice
- One small onion, finely chopped
- Two cloves garlic, minced
- 1 cup BBQ sauce (your favourite brand)
- 1 cup shredded cheddar cheese
- Salt and pepper to taste
- Chopped fresh parsley (for garnish, optional)

Directions:

1. Preheat your oven to 375°F (190°C).
2. Cut the bell peppers' tops off, removing the seeds and membranes. Rinse them under cold water and set them aside.
3. Cook the ground beef until it's no longer pink in a skillet over medium heat. Drain excess fat if needed.
4. Add chopped onions and minced garlic to the skillet with the ground beef. Cook until the onions are translucent and fragrant.

5. Stir in the cooked rice and BBQ sauce into the beef mixture. Season with salt and pepper to taste. Let it simmer for a few minutes until everything is well combined.

6. Stuff each bell pepper with the beef and rice mixture, pressing down gently to fill them completely.

7. Place the stuffed bell peppers upright in a baking dish. If needed, slice a small portion off the bottom of each pepper to make it stand straight.

8. Sprinkle shredded cheddar cheese over the tops of the stuffed peppers.

9. Cover the baking dish with aluminum foil and bake in the oven for 30-40 minutes or until the peppers are tender.

10. Remove the foil and bake for 5-10 minutes or until the cheese is melted and bubbly.

11. Once done, remove from the oven and let them cool for a few minutes before serving.

12. Optionally, garnish with chopped fresh parsley before serving.

Nutrition:

- **Calories:** Approximately 480 per serving
- **Total Fat:** 22g
- **Saturated Fat:** 9g
- **Cholesterol:** 90mg
- **Sodium:** 840mg
- **Total Carbohydrates:** 39g
- **Dietary Fiber:** 3g
- **Total Sugars:** 19g
- **Protein:** 30g

TRAEGER GRILLED VEGETABLE STIR-FRY

Cooking Time: 20 minutes
Servings: 4
Ingredients:

- 2 cups broccoli florets
- One red bell pepper, sliced
- One yellow bell pepper, sliced
- One zucchini, sliced
- One yellow squash, sliced
- 1 cup snap peas
- 1 cup mushrooms, sliced
- 2 tablespoons olive oil

- Three cloves garlic, minced
- 2 tablespoons soy sauce
- One tablespoon honey
- One teaspoon sesame oil
- Salt and pepper to taste
- Sesame seeds for garnish (optional)
- Cooked rice or noodles for serving

Directions:

1. Preheat your Traeger grill to medium-high heat (around 375°F/190°C).
2. In a large bowl, toss broccoli, bell peppers, zucchini, yellow squash, snap peas, and mushrooms with olive oil, minced garlic, soy sauce, honey, sesame oil, salt, and pepper until well coated.
3. Spread the vegetable mixture evenly on a grill tray or a grill-safe pan.
4. Place the tray or pan on the preheated grill and close the lid. Grill the vegetables for 10-15 minutes, stirring occasionally, until tender and slightly charred.
5. Once the vegetables are cooked through, remove them from the grill and transfer to a serving dish.
6. Garnish the stir-fry with sesame seeds if desired.
7. Serve the Traeger Grilled Vegetable Stir-Fry hot overcooked rice or noodles.

Nutrition: (per serving)

- Calories: 180
- Total Fat: 9g
- Saturated Fat: 1g
- Cholesterol: 0mg
- Sodium: 480mg
- Total Carbohydrate: 22g
- Dietary Fiber: 5g
- Sugars: 10g
- Protein: 6g

SMOKED MAPLE GLAZED HAM WITH BOURBON SAUCE

Cooking Time: 3 hours 30 minutes
Servings: 8-10
Ingredients:

- 1 (8-10 pound) bone-in smoked ham
- 1 cup maple syrup
- 1/4 cup brown sugar
- 1/4 cup Dijon mustard
- Two tablespoons apple cider vinegar
- One tablespoon Worcestershire sauce
- 1/2 teaspoon ground cloves
- 1/4 teaspoon ground cinnamon
- 1/4 teaspoon ground nutmeg
- 1/4 teaspoon black pepper
- 1/4 cup bourbon
- Two tablespoons butter
- Salt to taste

Directions:

1. **Prepare the Ham:** Preheat your smoker to 250°F (120°C). Place the smoked ham on the smoker rack and cook for about 2 hours or until the internal temperature reaches 140°F (60°C).

2. **Make the Maple Glaze:** In a saucepan, combine maple syrup, brown sugar, Dijon mustard, apple cider vinegar, Worcestershire sauce, ground cloves, cinnamon, nutmeg, and black pepper. Cook over medium heat, stirring occasionally, until the mixture thickens slightly, about 10-15 minutes.

3. **Glaze the Ham:** Once the ham reaches an internal temperature of 140°F (60°C), brush the maple glaze over the ham. Continue smoking for another 30 minutes, allowing the glaze to caramelize.

4. **Prepare the Bourbon Sauce:** Melt butter in a small saucepan over medium heat. Add bourbon and let it simmer for 2-3 minutes to cook off the alcohol. Remove from heat and set aside.

5. **Serve:** Remove the ham from the smoker and let it rest for 10-15 minutes before slicing. Serve the smoked maple glazed ham with the bourbon sauce on the side for drizzling.

Nutrition (per serving, based on eight servings):

- Calories: 600
- Total Fat: 21g
- Saturated Fat: 7g
- Cholesterol: 175mg
- Sodium: 2000mg
- Total Carbohydrate: 27g
- Dietary Fiber: 0g
- Sugars: 26g
- Protein: 62g

WOOD-FIRED LEMON HERB CHICKEN DRUMSTICKS

Cooking Time: 40 minutes

Servings: 4

Ingredients:

- Eight chicken drumsticks
- Two lemons, juiced and zested
- Three cloves garlic, minced
- Two tablespoons fresh rosemary, chopped
- Two tablespoons fresh thyme leaves
- One tablespoon olive oil
- Salt and pepper to taste

Directions:

1. **Marinate the Chicken:** In a large bowl, combine lemon juice, lemon zest, minced garlic, chopped rosemary, thyme leaves, olive oil, salt, and pepper. Add chicken drumsticks to the bowl and toss until they are evenly coated with the marinade. Cover the bowl and let the chicken marinate in the refrigerator for at least 30 minutes.

2. **Prepare the Wood-Fired Grill:** Preheat your wood-fired grill to medium-high heat (about 375-400°F/190-200°C). If using wood chips, soak them in water for about 30 minutes before grilling.

3. **Grill the Chicken:** Once the grill is hot, remove the chicken drumsticks from the marinade and shake off any excess. Place the drumsticks on the grill grate directly over the heat. Grill the chicken for about 20-25 minutes, turning occasionally, until they are cooked through and golden brown on all sides.

4. **Check for Doneness:** To ensure the chicken is fully cooked, use a meat thermometer to check the internal temperature of the drumsticks. They should register at least 165°F (75°C) when inserted into the thickest part of the meat without touching the bone.

5. **Serve:** Once the chicken drumsticks are cooked through, remove them from the grill and transfer them to a serving platter. Garnish with additional fresh herbs and lemon slices if desired. Serve hot and enjoy!

Nutrition:

NOTE: NUTRITION INFORMATION IS APPROXIMATE AND MAY VARY DEPENDING ON SPECIFIC INGREDIENTS AND PORTION SIZES.

- Calories: 280 kcal
- Protein: 32g
- Fat: 15g
- Carbohydrates: 4g
- Fiber: 1g
- Sugar: 1g
- Sodium: 400mg

GRILLED BBQ GLAZED MEATBALLS

Cooking Time: 40 minutes
Servings: 4
Ingredients:

- Eight chicken drumsticks
- 2 lemons, sliced
- Four cloves garlic, minced
- Two tablespoons fresh rosemary, chopped
- Two tablespoons fresh thyme, chopped
- 1/4 cup olive oil
- Salt and pepper to taste

Directions:

1. **Prepare the Wood Fire:** Prepare your wood-fired grill or oven for cooking. You'll want medium-high heat, around 375°F (190°C), with a combination of hardwood chunks for flavour.

2. **Marinate the Chicken:** In a large bowl, combine the olive oil, minced garlic, chopped rosemary, chopped thyme, salt, and pepper. Add the chicken drumsticks to the bowl and toss until they are well coated with the marinade. Allow the chicken to marinate for at least 30 minutes in the refrigerator.

3. **Prep the Grill:** Once ready, place the marinated drumsticks directly onto the grill grates. Arrange the lemon slices around the chicken on the grill.

4. **Grill the Chicken:** Grill the drumsticks for about 20-25 minutes, turning occasionally, until they are cooked and have a nice charred exterior. The internal temperature of the chicken should reach 165°F (74°C).

5. **Finish with Lemon:** During the last few minutes of grilling, squeeze some lemon juice over the drumsticks and place the lemon slices directly on top of the chicken for extra flavour.

6. **Serve:** Once the chicken is cooked, remove it from the grill and rest for a few minutes. Serve the wood-fired lemon herb chicken drumsticks hot, garnished with additional fresh herbs if desired.

Nutrition (per serving):

- Calories: 320
- Total Fat: 20g
- Saturated Fat: 4g
- Cholesterol: 120mg
- Sodium: 360mg
- Total Carbohydrate: 5g
- Dietary Fiber: 2g
- Sugars: 1g
- Protein: 28g

BBQ PORK TENDERLOIN WITH APPLE CHUTNEY

Cooking Time: 1 hour 30 minutes
Servings: 4
Ingredients:

- 1 lb pork tenderloin
- Salt and black pepper to taste
- One tablespoon olive oil
- 1 cup BBQ sauce
- Two large apples, peeled, cored, and diced
- One small red onion, finely chopped
- 1/4 cup apple cider vinegar
- 1/4 cup brown sugar
- 1/4 teaspoon ground cinnamon
- 1/4 teaspoon ground ginger

- Pinch of cloves

Directions:

1. Preheat your grill to medium-high heat.

2. Season the pork tenderloin generously with salt and black pepper.

3. Brush the pork tenderloin with olive oil to prevent sticking on the grill.

4. Place the pork tenderloin on the preheated grill and cook for about 20-25 minutes, turning occasionally, until the internal temperature reaches 145°F (63°C).

5. While the pork is grilling, prepare the apple chutney. Combine diced apples, red onion, apple cider vinegar, brown sugar, cinnamon, ginger, and cloves in a medium saucepan.

6. Bring the mixture to a simmer over medium heat, then reduce the heat to low and let it cook for about 20-25 minutes, stirring occasionally, until the apples are tender and the chutney has thickened slightly.

7. Once the pork is cooked, remove it from the grill and rest for 5-10 minutes before slicing.

8. Slice the pork tenderloin into thick slices and serve with a generous spoonful of apple chutney on top.

Nutrition (per serving):

- Calories: 350 kcal

- Protein: 25g

- Carbohydrates: 35g

- Fat: 12g

- Fiber: 4g

- Sugar: 25g

- Sodium: 600mg

TRAEGER SMOKED STUFFED PEPPERS WITH ITALIAN SAUSAGE

Cooking Time: 1 hour 30 minutes
Servings: 4
Ingredients:

- Four large bell peppers, any colour

- 1 pound Italian sausage, mild or hot

- 1 cup cooked rice

- One small onion, diced

- Two cloves garlic, minced

- 1 cup shredded mozzarella cheese

- One can (14.5 oz) diced tomatoes, drained

- One teaspoon Italian seasoning
- Salt and pepper to taste
- Olive oil

Directions:

1. **Preheat the Traeger Grill:** Follow the manufacturer's instructions to preheat your Traeger grill to 375°F (190°C).

2. **Prepare the Peppers:** Cut the tops off the bell peppers and remove the seeds and membranes. Lightly brush the outside of the peppers with olive oil.

3. **Prepare the Filling:** In a skillet over medium heat, cook the Italian sausage until browned and cooked through, breaking it apart with a spoon as it cooks. Remove excess grease if needed. Add diced onions and minced garlic to the skillet and cook until softened about 3-4 minutes.

4. **Combine Ingredients:** In a large mixing bowl, combine the cooked Italian sausage mixture with cooked rice, diced tomatoes, Italian seasoning, half of the shredded mozzarella cheese, salt, and pepper. Mix well until all ingredients are evenly distributed.

5. **Stuff the Peppers:** Stuff each prepared bell pepper with the sausage and rice mixture, pressing down gently to fill them. Place the stuffed peppers upright in a baking dish or directly on the Traeger grill grate.

6. **Smoke the Peppers:** Place the baking dish with the stuffed peppers on the preheated Traeger grill. Close the lid and smoke for 45-60 minutes or until the peppers are tender and slightly charred on the edges.

7. **Add Cheese:** About 10 minutes before the peppers are done, sprinkle the remaining shredded mozzarella cheese over the tops of the peppers and allow it to melt and bubble.

8. **Serve:** Carefully remove the cheese from the grill once the cheese is melted and the peppers are cooked through. Let them cool for a few minutes before serving.

Nutrition: NOTE: NUTRITION INFORMATION MAY VARY DEPENDING ON THE INGREDIENTS USED.

- Calories: 480 kcal
- Fat: 31g
- Carbohydrates: 23g
- Protein: 27g
- Fiber: 3g
- Sugar: 5g
- Sodium: 900mg

WOOD-FIRED SPICY GARLIC SHRIMP LINGUINE

Cooking Time: 25 minutes

Servings: 4

Ingredients:

- 12 oz linguine pasta
- 1 lb large shrimp, peeled and deveined
- Four cloves garlic, minced
- Two tablespoons olive oil
- One teaspoon red pepper flakes (adjust to taste)
- One teaspoon paprika
- One teaspoon dried oregano
- Salt to taste
- Freshly ground black pepper to taste
- 1/4 cup chopped fresh parsley
- One lemon, zest and juice
- Grated Parmesan cheese (optional for serving)

Directions:

1. Preheat your wood-fired oven to 400°F (200°C).
2. Cook the linguine pasta according to package instructions until al dente. Drain and set aside, reserving about 1/2 cup of pasta water.
3. Combine the shrimp, minced garlic, olive oil, red pepper flakes, paprika, dried oregano, salt, and black pepper in a large mixing bowl. Toss until the shrimp are evenly coated.
4. Place the seasoned shrimp on a baking sheet in the preheated wood-fired oven. Cook for 5-7 minutes or until the shrimp are pink and cooked. Be careful not to overcook them.
5. Heat a tablespoon of olive oil over medium heat in a large skillet or pan. Add the cooked linguine, roasted shrimp, chopped parsley, lemon zest, and lemon juice. Toss everything together gently, adding reserved pasta water to loosen the pasta and create a sauce.
6. Once everything is heated through and well combined, remove from heat.
7. Serve the wood-fired spicy garlic shrimp linguine hot, garnished with additional chopped parsley and grated Parmesan cheese if desired.

Nutrition: (PER SERVING)

Calories: 410 kcal

Total Fat: 10g

- Saturated Fat: 1.5g
- Cholesterol: 180mg
- Sodium: 300mg
- Total Carbohydrates: 50g
- Dietary Fiber: 3g

- Sugars: 2g
- Protein: 30g

SMOKED BBQ BEEF SHORT RIBS WITH BEER BARBECUE SAUCE

Cooking Time: 6 hours
Servings: 4-6
Ingredients:
For the Beef Short Ribs:

- 4-6 beef short ribs
- Two tablespoons olive oil
- Salt and pepper to taste
- One tablespoon paprika
- One tablespoon garlic powder
- One tablespoon onion powder

For the Beer Barbecue Sauce:

- 1 cup ketchup
- ½ cup beer (stout or ale works well)
- ¼ cup apple cider vinegar
- Two tablespoons brown sugar
- Two tablespoons Worcestershire sauce
- 1 tablespoon Dijon mustard
- One teaspoon smoked paprika
- Salt and pepper to taste

Directions:

1. **Prepare the Beef Short Ribs:** Preheat your smoker to 225°F (110°C). Rub the beef short ribs with olive oil and season them generously with salt, pepper, paprika, garlic powder, and onion powder.

2. **Smoke the Ribs:** Place the seasoned beef short ribs on the smoker grate and smoke for about 4-5 hours, or until the internal temperature reaches 203°F (95°C) and the meat is tender and has a rich smoky flavour.

3. **Make the Beer Barbecue Sauce:** In a saucepan over medium heat, combine ketchup, beer, apple cider vinegar, brown sugar, Worcestershire sauce, Dijon mustard, smoked paprika, salt, and pepper. Stir well to combine and bring to a simmer. Let the sauce cook for about 15-20 minutes, stirring occasionally, until it thickens slightly.

4. **Glaze the Ribs:** During the last hour of smoking, baste the beef short ribs with the beer barbecue sauce every 15 minutes, allowing the sauce to caramelize and form a delicious glaze on the ribs.

5. **Serve:** Once the beef short ribs are fully cooked and glazed, remove them from the smoker and rest for a few minutes. Serve the ribs hot, with extra beer barbecue sauce on the side for dipping.

Nutrition:

NUTRITIONAL INFORMATION PER SERVING (ASSUMING SIX SERVINGS):

- Calories: 480
- Total Fat: 28g
- Saturated Fat: 10g
- Cholesterol: 120mg
- Sodium: 920mg
- Total Carbohydrates: 19g
- Dietary Fiber: 1g
- Sugars: 15g
- Protein: 34g

TRAEGER GRILLED JALAPENO POPPERS WITH CREAM CHEESE

Cooking Time: 25 minutes
Servings: 6
Ingredients:

- 12 large jalapeno peppers
- 8 ounces cream cheese, softened
- 1 cup shredded cheddar cheese
- Six slices of bacon, cut in half
- One teaspoon garlic powder
- One teaspoon onion powder
- 1/2 teaspoon paprika
- Salt and pepper to taste
- Toothpicks

Directions:

1. Preheat your Traeger grill to 375°F (190°C).

2. Cut the jalapeno peppers in half lengthwise. Using a small spoon or knife, remove the seeds and membranes, being careful to keep the pepper halves intact.

3. Combine the softened cream cheese, shredded cheddar cheese, garlic powder, onion powder, paprika, salt, and pepper in a mixing bowl. Mix until well combined.

4. Fill each jalapeno half with the cream cheese mixture, pressing it in gently.

5. Wrap each stuffed jalapeno half with a half-slice of bacon and secure with a toothpick.

6. Place the bacon-wrapped jalapeno poppers directly on the grill grates of your Traeger.

7. Grill the poppers for about 20-25 minutes until the bacon is crispy, and the peppers are tender, turning once halfway through cooking.

8. Once cooked, carefully remove the jalapeno poppers from the grill and let them cool for a few minutes before serving.

Nutrition:

NOTE: NUTRITIONAL VALUES ARE APPROXIMATE AND MAY VARY DEPENDING ON SPECIFIC INGREDIENTS.

- Calories: 270 kcal
- Total Fat: 22g
  - Saturated Fat: 12g
  - Trans Fat: 0g
- Cholesterol: 65mg
- Sodium: 420mg
- Total Carbohydrates: 6g
  - Dietary Fiber: 1g
  - Sugars: 3g
- Protein: 11g

Wood-Fired BBQ Meatballs with Sweet and Spicy Sauce

Cooking Time: 30 minutes
Servings: 4-6
Ingredients:
For the meatballs:

- 1 pound ground beef
- 1/2 cup breadcrumbs
- 1/4 cup grated Parmesan cheese
- 1/4 cup finely chopped onion
- One clove garlic, minced
- One egg
- Salt and pepper to taste

For the sauce:

- 1 cup ketchup
- 1/4 cup brown sugar
- Two tablespoons apple cider vinegar
- One tablespoon Worcestershire sauce
- One teaspoon smoked paprika
- 1/2 teaspoon chilli powder
- 1/4 teaspoon cayenne pepper (adjust to taste for spiciness)

Directions:

1. **Preheat the Wood-Fired Oven:** Preheat your wood-fired oven to 400°F (200°C) and prepare it for direct cooking.

2. **Make the Meatballs:** In a large mixing bowl, combine the ground beef, breadcrumbs, Parmesan cheese, onion, garlic, egg, salt, and pepper. Mix well until everything is evenly incorporated. Shape the mixture into meatballs about 1 inch in diameter.

3. **Cook the Meatballs:** Place the meatballs directly on the grill grate of the wood-fired oven. Cook for about 15-20 minutes, turning occasionally, until they are browned and cooked through.

4. **Prepare the Sauce:** While the meatballs are cooking, prepare the sauce. Combine the ketchup, brown sugar, apple cider vinegar, Worcestershire sauce, smoked paprika, chilli powder, and cayenne pepper in a small saucepan. Cook over medium heat, stirring constantly, until the sugar is dissolved and the sauce is heated about 5-7 minutes.

5. **Coat the Meatballs:** Transfer them to a large mixing bowl once the meatballs are cooked. Pour the sauce over the meatballs and toss gently to coat them evenly.

6. **Serve:** Arrange the BBQ meatballs on a platter and serve hot. If desired, garnish with chopped parsley or sliced green onions.

Nutrition:

- NOTE: NUTRITIONAL VALUES ARE APPROXIMATE AND MAY VARY DEPENDING ON SPECIFIC INGREDIENTS.
- **Calories:** 320 kcal
- **Protein:** 20g
- **Fat:** 15g
- **Carbohydrates:** 25g
- **Fiber:** 1g
- **Sugar:** 15g
- **Sodium:** 800mg

SMOKED BUFFALO CHICKEN DIP WITH TORTILLA CHIPS

Cooking Time: 1 hour
Servings: 6-8
Ingredients:

- 2 cups shredded cooked chicken (smoked chicken works best)
- 1 cup cream cheese, softened
- 1 cup shredded mozzarella cheese
- 1 cup shredded cheddar cheese
- 1/2 cup buffalo sauce
- 1/4 cup ranch dressing
- 1/4 cup sour cream
- 1/4 cup chopped green onions (optional)
- Tortilla chips for serving

Directions:

1. Preheat your smoker to 225°F (107°C).
2. Combine the shredded chicken, cream cheese, mozzarella cheese, cheddar cheese, buffalo sauce, ranch dressing, sour cream, and chopped green onions in a mixing bowl. Mix until well combined.
3. Transfer the mixture to a cast-iron skillet or a disposable aluminium pan.
4. Place the skillet or pan in the smoker and smoke for 30-40 minutes or until the dip is heated and bubbly.
5. Once done, remove the skillet or pan from the smoker and let it cool slightly.
6. Garnish with additional chopped green onions if desired.
7. Serve the smoked buffalo chicken dip warm with tortilla chips for dipping.

Nutrition:

- **Calories:** 320 kcal
- **Fat:** 25g

- **Saturated Fat:** 12g
- **Cholesterol:** 90mg
- **Sodium:** 790mg
- **Carbohydrates:** 5g
- **Fiber:** 0.5g
- **Sugar:** 1g
- **Protein:** 20g

GRILLED BACON-WRAPPED ASPARAGUS SPEARS

Cooking Time: 20 minutes
Servings: 4
Ingredients:

- 1 pound fresh asparagus spears, trimmed
- 8 slices bacon
- Olive oil (for brushing)
- Salt and pepper to taste

Directions:

1. Preheat your grill to medium-high heat.
2. Divide the asparagus spears into four bundles, about 5-6 each.
3. Wrap two slices of bacon around each bundle of asparagus, ensuring the spears are fully covered.
4. Secure the bacon with toothpicks if necessary.
5. Brush the bacon-wrapped asparagus bundles lightly with olive oil and season with salt and pepper.
6. Place the bundles directly onto the preheated grill.
7. Grill for 10-12 minutes, turning occasionally, until the bacon is crispy and the asparagus is tender.
8. Remove from the grill and let cool slightly before serving.

Nutrition:

- Calories: 215 kcal
- Fat: 18g
- Saturated Fat: 6g
- Cholesterol: 29mg
- Sodium: 390mg
- Carbohydrates: 2g

- Fiber: 1g
- Sugars: 1g
- Protein: 11g

BBQ CHICKEN WINGS WITH HONEY SRIRACHA GLAZE

Cooking Time: 45 minutes

Servings: 4

Ingredients:

- 2 lbs chicken wings
- Salt and pepper to taste
- 1/2 cup barbecue sauce
- 1/4 cup honey
- Two tablespoons Sriracha sauce
- Two cloves garlic, minced
- One tablespoon soy sauce
- One tablespoon olive oil
- One tablespoon chopped fresh cilantro (optional, for garnish)
- Sesame seeds (optional, for garnish)

Directions:

1. Preheat your oven to 400°F (200°C). Line a baking sheet with parchment paper or aluminium foil for easy cleanup.

2. Whisk together barbecue sauce, honey, Sriracha sauce, minced garlic, and soy sauce in a small bowl. Set aside.

3. Pat the chicken wings dry with paper towels and season them generously with salt and pepper.

4. In a large bowl, toss the chicken wings with olive oil until evenly coated.

5. Arrange the chicken wings on the prepared baking sheet in a single layer, making sure they don't touch.

6. Bake the chicken wings in the preheated oven for 25-30 minutes or until crispy, flipping them halfway through cooking.

7. Once the wings are cooked, remove them from the oven and transfer them to a large mixing bowl.

8. Pour the prepared honey Sriracha glaze over the hot chicken wings and toss them until they are evenly coated.

9. Return the glazed wings to the baking sheet and broil them for 2-3 minutes, or until the glaze is sticky and caramelized, watching closely to prevent burning.

10. Remove the wings from the oven and transfer them to a serving platter. Sprinkle with chopped fresh cilantro and sesame seeds if desired.

11. Serve the BBQ chicken wings with honey Sriracha glaze immediately, and enjoy!

Nutrition:

- CALORIES: 350 kcal
- TOTAL FAT: 18g
- SATURATED FAT: 5g
- CHOLESTEROL: 90mg
- SODIUM: 650mg
- TOTAL CARBOHYDRATES: 24g
- DIETARY FIBER: 1g
- SUGARS: 20g
- PROTEIN: 23g

TRAEGER SMOKED DEVILED EGGS WITH BACON

Cooking Time: 45 minutes
Servings: 12
Ingredients:

- Six large eggs
- Three slices of bacon
- 1/4 cup mayonnaise
- Two teaspoons Dijon mustard
- One teaspoon white vinegar
- Salt and pepper to taste
- Smoked paprika, for garnish
- Chopped chives for garnish

Directions:

1. **Preheat your Traeger grill to 225°F (107°C) according to the manufacturer's instructions.**

2. Place the eggs directly on the grill grate and smoke for 30 minutes.

3. While the eggs are smoking, cook the bacon in a skillet over medium heat until crispy. Transfer to a paper towel-lined plate to drain excess grease. Once cooled, chop the bacon into small pieces.

4. After smoking, carefully remove the eggs from the grill and place them in a bowl of ice water to cool for 10 minutes.

5. Peel the eggs and slice them in half lengthwise. Gently scoop out the yolks and place them in a separate bowl.

6. Mash the egg yolks with a fork until smooth. Add mayonnaise, Dijon mustard, white vinegar, salt, and pepper. Mix until well combined.

7. Spoon or pipe the yolk mixture back into the egg whites.

8. Top each deviled egg with chopped bacon, smoked paprika, and chopped chives.

9. Arrange the deviled eggs on a serving platter and serve immediately.

Nutrition: NOTE: NUTRITION INFORMATION MAY VARY DEPENDING ON THE INGREDIENTS USED.

- Calories: 94
- Total Fat: 8g
- Saturated Fat: 2g
- Cholesterol: 101mg
- Sodium: 150mg
- Total Carbohydrates: 1g
- Dietary Fiber: 0g
- Sugars: 0g
- Protein: 4g

WOOD-FIRED SPINACH AND ARTICHOKE DIP

Cooking Time: 30 minutes
Servings: 6-8
Ingredients:

- One tablespoon olive oil
- 2 cloves garlic, minced
- One small onion, finely chopped
- 1 (10-ounce) package of frozen chopped spinach, thawed and drained

- 1 (14-ounce) can artichoke hearts, drained and chopped
- 8 ounces cream cheese, softened
- 1/2 cup mayonnaise
- 1/2 cup sour cream
- 1 cup shredded mozzarella cheese
- 1/2 cup grated Parmesan cheese
- Salt and pepper to taste
- Wood chips for smoking (optional)

Directions:

1. Preheat your wood-fired grill or oven to 375°F (190°C).

2. In a skillet, heat olive oil over medium heat. Add minced garlic, chopped onion, and sauté until softened and fragrant, about 3-4 minutes.

3. Stir in the chopped spinach and artichoke hearts. Cook for another 2-3 minutes until heated through.

4. Combine the softened cream cheese, mayonnaise, and sour cream in a mixing bowl until smooth.

5. Add the cooked spinach and artichoke mixture to the bowl, shredded mozzarella and grated Parmesan cheese. Mix until well combined—season with salt and pepper to taste.

6. If using a wood-fired grill, spread soaked wood chips over the coals to create smoke. Place the dip in a heatproof dish suitable for grilling.

7. Place the dish on the grill grate and close the lid. Cook for 15-20 minutes until the dip is bubbly and golden brown.

8. If using an oven, transfer the mixture to a baking dish and bake for 20-25 minutes until heated and bubbly.

9. Serve hot with tortilla chips, crackers, or sliced baguette.

Nutrition: (PER SERVING, BASED ON SIX SERVINGS)

Calories: 320

Total Fat: 26g

- Saturated Fat: 12g
- Trans Fat: 0g
- Cholesterol: 60mg
- Sodium: 550mg
- Total Carbohydrates: 10g
- Dietary Fiber: 3g
- Sugars: 2g
- Protein: 12g

GRILLED TERIYAKI CHICKEN SKEWERS WITH PINEAPPLE

Cooking Time: 30 minutes

Servings: 4

Ingredients:

- 1 pound boneless, skinless chicken breasts, cut into 1-inch cubes
- 1 cup pineapple chunks
- ½ cup teriyaki sauce
- Two tablespoons soy sauce
- Two tablespoons honey
- One tablespoon olive oil
- One teaspoon minced garlic
- Wooden skewers, soaked in water for 30 minutes

Directions:

1. To create the marinade, mix teriyaki sauce, soy sauce, honey, olive oil, and minced garlic in a bowl.

2. Place the chicken cubes in a resealable plastic bag or shallow dish. Pour half the marinade over the chicken, reserving the rest for basting. Seal the bag or cover the dish and refrigerate for at least 30 minutes to marinate.

3. Preheat your grill to medium-high heat.

4. Thread the marinated chicken and pineapple chunks alternately onto the soaked wooden skewers.

5. Place the skewers on the preheated grill and cook for 8-10 minutes, turning occasionally, or until the chicken is cooked and the pineapple is caramelized.

6. While grilling, baste the skewers with the reserved marinade to enhance flavour.

7. Once cooked, remove the skewers from the grill and let them rest for a few minutes before serving.

8. Serve hot, garnished with sesame seeds and chopped green onions if desired.

Nutrition:

- Calories: 280 kcal
- Total Fat: 7g
- Saturated Fat: 1.5g

- Cholesterol: 80mg
- Sodium: 1050mg
- Total Carbohydrate: 23g
- Dietary Fiber: 1g
- Sugars: 18g
- Protein: 30g

SMOKED CHEDDAR AND BACON STUFFED MUSHROOMS

Cooking Time: 30 minutes
Servings: 4
Ingredients:

- 16 large mushrooms, stems removed and reserved
- Six slices of bacon, cooked until crispy and crumbled
- 1 cup smoked cheddar cheese, grated
- Two cloves garlic, minced
- Two tablespoons fresh parsley, finely chopped
- Two tablespoons olive oil
- Salt and pepper to taste

Directions:

1. Preheat your oven to 375°F (190°C).
2. Clean the mushrooms with a damp cloth and remove the stems. Finely chop the mushroom stems and set aside.
3. In a skillet, heat the olive oil over medium heat. Add the minced garlic and chopped mushroom stems. Sauté until softened, about 3-4 minutes.
4. Combine the sautéed mushroom stems and garlic in a mixing bowl with the crumbled bacon, smoked cheddar cheese, and fresh parsley. Mix well to combine.
5. Season the mushroom caps with salt and pepper. Stuff each mushroom cap generously with the bacon and cheese mixture, pressing down gently to pack it in.
6. Place the stuffed mushrooms on a baking sheet lined with parchment paper.
7. Bake in the oven for 15-20 minutes or until the mushrooms are tender and the cheese is melted and bubbly.
8. Once done, remove from the oven and let them cool slightly before serving.
9. Serve the smoked cheddar and bacon stuffed mushrooms warm as a delicious appetizer or side dish.

Nutrition:

- **Calories:** 240 kcal
- **Total Fat:** 18g
- **Saturated Fat:** 7g
- **Cholesterol:** 35mg
- **Sodium:** 400mg
- **Total Carbohydrates:** 5g
- **Dietary Fiber:** 1g
- **Sugars:** 2g
- **Protein:** 14g

BBQ PULLED PORK NACHOS WITH QUESO

Cooking Time: 2 hours
Servings: 6-8
Ingredients:

- 1 pound pork shoulder or butt, trimmed of excess fat
- 1 cup BBQ sauce of your choice
- One bag tortilla chips
- 1 cup shredded cheddar cheese
- 1 cup shredded Monterey Jack cheese
- 1/2 cup diced red onion
- 1/4 cup chopped fresh cilantro
- One jalapeño, thinly sliced (optional)
- One avocado, diced (optional)
- Sour cream for garnish (optional)

Queso Ingredients:

- Two tablespoons butter
- Two tablespoons all-purpose flour
- 1 cup milk
- 1 cup shredded cheddar cheese
- 1/2 cup shredded Monterey Jack cheese
- 1/4 teaspoon garlic powder
- Salt and pepper to taste

Directions:

1. **Prepare the Pork:** Season the pork shoulder with salt and pepper. Please place it in a slow cooker and pour the BBQ sauce over the top. Cook on low for 8 hours or high for 4 hours until the pork is tender and quickly shreds with a fork. Once cooked, shred the pork using two forks.

2. **Make the Queso:** Melt the butter over medium heat in a saucepan. Stir in the flour and cook for 1-2 minutes until it forms a paste. Gradually whisk in the milk until smooth. Cook, stirring constantly, until the mixture thickens, about 3-4 minutes. Reduce the heat to low and stir in the shredded cheddar and Monterey Jack cheeses until melted and smooth— season with garlic powder, salt, and pepper. Keep warm until ready to use.

3. **Assemble the Nachos:** Preheat the oven to 350°F (175°C). Spread the tortilla chips in a single layer on a large baking sheet or oven-safe dish. Sprinkle half of the shredded cheddar and Monterey Jack cheeses over the chips. Top with the shredded BBQ pork, diced red onion, and remaining cheese.

4. **Bake:** Place the nachos in the oven and bake for 10-15 minutes until the cheese is melted and bubbly.

5. **Serve:** Remove the nachos from the oven and drizzle with the prepared queso. Garnish with chopped cilantro, sliced jalapeños, diced avocado, and sour cream if desired. Serve immediately.

Nutrition:

(Note: Nutritional values may vary depending on ingredients used and portion sizes)

- Calories: Approximately 450 per serving
- Protein: Approximately 20g per serving
- Fat: Approximately 25g per serving
- Carbohydrates: Approximately 35g per serving
- Fiber: Approximately 4g per serving

TRAEGER GRILLED BRUSCHETTA WITH TOMATO AND BASIL

Cooking Time: 15 minutes
Servings: 4
Ingredients:

- Four large ripe tomatoes, diced
- 1/4 cup fresh basil leaves, chopped
- Two cloves garlic, minced
- Two tablespoons extra virgin olive oil
- One tablespoon balsamic vinegar
- Salt and pepper to taste
- 1 French baguette, sliced diagonally

- Two tablespoons grated Parmesan cheese (optional)

Directions:

1. Preheat your Traeger grill to 375°F (190°C) according to the manufacturer's instructions.

2. Combine diced tomatoes, chopped basil, minced garlic, olive oil, balsamic vinegar, salt, and pepper in a bowl. Mix well and set aside to marinate.

3. Place the sliced baguette on the grill grates for about 2-3 minutes per side until lightly toasted and grill marks appear.

4. Remove the toasted baguette slices from the grill and arrange them on a serving platter.

5. Spoon the tomato and basil mixture generously over each toasted baguette slice.

6. If desired, sprinkle grated Parmesan cheese over the top of each bruschetta.

7. Serve immediately and enjoy!

Nutrition: NOTE: NUTRITION INFORMATION IS APPROXIMATE AND MAY VARY DEPENDING ON INGREDIENTS.

- Calories: 220 kcal
- Total Fat: 8g
  - Saturated Fat: 1.5g
  - Trans Fat: 0g
- Cholesterol: 0mg
- Sodium: 320mg
- Total Carbohydrate: 32g
  - Dietary Fiber: 3g
  - Sugars: 3g
- Protein: 6g

WOOD-FIRED MINI BEEF SLIDERS WITH CHIPOTLE MAYO

Cooking Time: 25 minutes
Servings: 4
Ingredients:
For the sliders:

- 1 pound ground beef
- 1/2 teaspoon salt
- 1/4 teaspoon black pepper
- 1/2 teaspoon garlic powder
- 1/2 teaspoon onion powder
- Eight small slider buns

For the Chipotle mayo:

- 1/2 cup mayonnaise
- One chipotle pepper in adobo sauce, minced
- One teaspoon adobo sauce (from the chipotle pepper can)
- One clove garlic, minced
- One tablespoon lime juice
- Salt to taste

For garnish (optional):

- Lettuce leaves
- Sliced tomatoes
- Sliced red onion

Directions:

1. Preheat your wood-fired grill to medium-high heat.
2. Combine ground beef, salt, black pepper, garlic powder, and onion powder in a mixing bowl. Mix well until the seasonings are evenly distributed.
3. Divide the seasoned ground beef into eight equal portions. Shape each portion into a small patty, about the size of your slider buns.
4. Place the patties on the preheated grill and cook for about 3-4 minutes per side until they reach your desired level of doneness.
5. While the sliders are cooking, prepare the chipotle mayo. In a small bowl, mix mayonnaise, minced chipotle pepper, adobo sauce, minced garlic, lime juice, and salt to taste. Adjust the seasoning according to your preference.
6. Once the sliders are cooked, remove them from the grill and rest for a few minutes.
7. Slice the slider buns in half and lightly toast them on the grill.
8. To assemble the sliders, spread a generous amount of chipotle mayo on the bottom half of each bun. Place a slider patty on top of the mayo, then add optional garnishes like lettuce, tomato slices, and red onion slices if desired. Top with the other half of the bun.
9. Serve the wood-fired mini beef sliders immediately, and enjoy!

Nutrition: (NUTRITIONAL VALUES ARE APPROXIMATE AND MAY VARY DEPENDING ON INGREDIENTS AND PORTION SIZES.)

- Calories: 380 kcal
- Protein: 20g
- Fat: 26g
- Carbohydrates: 17g
- Fiber: 1g
- Sugar: 2g
- Sodium: 710mg

SMOKED CAJUN GARLIC BUTTER SHRIMP

Cooking Time: 20 minutes

Servings: 4

Ingredients:

- 1 pound large shrimp, peeled and deveined
- Four tablespoons unsalted butter, melted
- Four cloves garlic, minced
- One tablespoon smoked paprika
- One teaspoon cayenne pepper
- One teaspoon dried thyme
- One teaspoon dried oregano
- Salt and pepper to taste
- Fresh parsley, chopped (for garnish)
- Lemon wedges (for serving)

Directions:

1. Preheat your grill or smoker to medium-high heat, around 350°F (175°C).
2. In a small bowl, mix melted butter, minced garlic, smoked paprika, cayenne pepper, dried thyme, oregano, salt, and pepper.
3. Place the shrimp in a large bowl and pour the prepared butter mixture over them. Toss until the shrimp are evenly coated.
4. Thread the shrimp onto skewers, leaving a little space between each shrimp.
5. Place the shrimp skewers on the preheated grill or smoker. Cook for 2-3 minutes per side until the shrimp are pink and opaque.
6. Once cooked, remove the shrimp skewers from the grill and transfer them to a serving platter.
7. Garnish with chopped fresh parsley and serve with lemon wedges on the side.

Nutrition (per serving):

- Calories: 240
- Fat: 14g
- Saturated Fat: 7g
- Cholesterol: 240mg
- Sodium: 550mg
- Carbohydrates: 3g
- Fiber: 1g

- Sugar: 0g
- Protein: 24g

GRILLED BBQ POTATO SKINS WITH CHEESE AND BACON

Cooking Time: 45 minutes
Servings: 4
Ingredients:

- Four large russet potatoes
- 1 cup shredded cheddar cheese
- Six slices bacon, cooked and crumbled
- 1/4 cup BBQ sauce
- Two green onions, thinly sliced
- Salt and pepper to taste
- Sour cream (optional for serving)
- Chopped fresh parsley or cilantro (optional, for garnish)

Directions:

1. Preheat your grill to medium-high heat.
2. Wash the potatoes thoroughly and pat them dry with paper towels.
3. Pierce each potato several times with a fork to allow steam to escape during cooking.
4. Microwave the potatoes on high for about 5 minutes per potato or until they are just slightly tender when pierced with a fork. Alternatively, depending on their size, you can bake the potatoes in a preheated oven at 400°F (200°C) for about 45-60 minutes.
5. Once the potatoes are cooked, let them cool slightly until they are safe to handle.
6. Slice each potato in half lengthwise. Use a spoon to scoop out the flesh, leaving about 1/4 inch of flesh attached to the skin. Save the scooped-out potato flesh for another use, such as mashed potatoes.
7. Brush the inside and outside of each potato skin with BBQ sauce.
8. Season the inside of each potato skin with salt and pepper to taste.
9. Place the potato skins on the preheated grill, skin side down. Grill 5-7 minutes or until they crisp up and develop grill marks.
10. Flip the potato skins over using tongs. Fill each skin with shredded cheddar cheese and crumbled bacon.
11. Close the lid and continue grilling for another 5-7 minutes until the cheese is melted and bubbly.
12. Carefully remove the potato skins from the grill using tongs and transfer them to a serving platter.

13. Garnish the potato skins with sliced green onions and chopped parsley or cilantro, if desired.

14. Serve the grilled BBQ potato skins hot, with sour cream on the side for dipping if desired.

Nutrition (per serving):

- Calories: 380
- Total Fat: 18g
  - Saturated Fat: 8g
- Cholesterol: 40mg
- Sodium: 720mg
- Total Carbohydrates: 40g
  - Dietary Fiber: 4g
  - Sugars: 8g
- Protein: 16g

TRAEGER SMOKED SWEET POTATO FRIES WITH GARLIC AIOLI

Cooking Time: 1 hour 15 minutes

Servings: 4

Ingredients:

For Sweet Potato Fries:

- Four large sweet potatoes, peeled and cut into fries
- Two tablespoons olive oil
- One teaspoon smoked paprika
- 1 teaspoon garlic powder
- One teaspoon onion powder
- Salt and pepper to taste

For Garlic Aioli:

- 1/2 cup mayonnaise
- Two cloves garlic, minced
- One tablespoon lemon juice
- Salt and pepper to taste

Directions:

1. **Preheat Traeger Grill:** Preheat your Traeger grill to 375°F (190°C) according to the manufacturer's instructions.

2. **Prepare Sweet Potato Fries:** In a large bowl, toss sweet potato fries with olive oil, smoked paprika, garlic powder, onion powder, salt, and pepper until evenly coated.

3. **Smoke Sweet Potato Fries:** Place the seasoned sweet potato fries directly on the grill grates and smoke for about 45 minutes to 1 hour, or until they are tender and lightly browned, turning occasionally for even cooking.

4. **Make Garlic Aioli:** While the fries are smoking, prepare the garlic aioli. Mix mayonnaise, minced garlic, lemon juice, salt, and pepper in a small bowl until well combined. Adjust seasoning to taste.

5. **Serve:** Once the sweet potato fries are done, remove them from the grill and serve hot with the prepared garlic aioli for dipping.

Nutrition: (NUTRITIONAL VALUES ARE APPROXIMATE AND WILL VARY DEPENDING ON SERVING SIZE AND SPECIFIC INGREDIENTS USED)

- Calories: 320 kcal
- Fat: 18g
- Carbohydrates: 35g
- Fiber: 5g
- Protein: 3g

WOOD-FIRED SPICY BUFFALO CAULIFLOWER BITES

Cooking Time: 30 minutes
Servings: 4
Ingredients:

- One head of cauliflower, cut into bite-sized florets
- 1 cup all-purpose flour
- 1 cup water
- One teaspoon garlic powder
- One teaspoon onion powder
- One teaspoon paprika
- Salt and pepper to taste
- 1 cup hot sauce (such as Frank's RedHot)
- 1/4 cup unsalted butter, melted
- One tablespoon honey (optional)
- Cooking spray

Directions:

1. Preheat your wood-fired oven to 450°F (230°C).

2. Mix the flour, water, garlic powder, onion powder, paprika, salt, and pepper in a bowl until you have a smooth batter.

3. Dip each cauliflower floret into the batter, coating it completely, then place it on a baking sheet lined with parchment paper.

4. Once all cauliflower florets are coated, lightly spray them with cooking spray.

5. Place the baking sheet in the preheated wood-fired oven and cook for 15-20 minutes until the cauliflower is tender and the batter is golden brown, turning halfway through.

6. In a separate bowl, mix the hot sauce, melted butter, and honey (if using) to make the buffalo sauce.

7. Once the cauliflower is cooked, please remove it from the oven and transfer it to a large mixing bowl.

8. Pour the buffalo sauce over the cauliflower florets and toss until they are evenly coated.

9. Return the coated cauliflower to the baking sheet and place it back in the wood-fired oven for 5-7 minutes, until the sauce bubbles and the cauliflower is crisp.

10. Remove from the oven and let cool for a few minutes before serving.

11. Enjoy your wood-fired spicy buffalo cauliflower bites as a delicious appetizer or snack!

Nutrition:

- Serving Size: 1/4 of recipe
- Calories: 240
- Total Fat: 9g
- Saturated Fat: 5g
- Cholesterol: 20mg
- Sodium: 1800mg
- Total Carbohydrates: 34g
- Dietary Fiber: 3g
- Sugars: 5g
- Protein: 6g

BBQ CHICKEN TAQUITOS WITH AVOCADO RANCH DIPPING SAUCE

Cooking Time: 30 minutes
Servings: 4
Ingredients:
For the Taquitos:

- 2 cups shredded cooked chicken
- 1 cup BBQ sauce
- 1 cup shredded cheddar cheese
- 1/4 cup chopped green onions

- 8-10 small flour tortillas
- Cooking spray

For the Avocado Ranch Dipping Sauce:

- One ripe avocado
- 1/2 cup Greek yogurt
- 1/4 cup mayonnaise
- One tablespoon ranch seasoning mix
- One tablespoon lime juice
- Salt and pepper to taste

Directions:

1. Preheat your oven to 375°F (190°C).
2. Combine shredded chicken and BBQ sauce in a mixing bowl until well coated.
3. Lay out a tortilla and spoon a generous amount of the BBQ chicken mixture onto one end. Sprinkle with shredded cheddar cheese and chopped green onions.
4. Roll up the tortilla tightly and place it seam-side down on a baking sheet lined with parchment paper. Repeat with the remaining tortillas and filling.
5. Lightly spray the tops of the taquitos with cooking spray. This will help them crisp up in the oven.
6. Bake in the oven for 15-20 minutes or until the taquitos are golden and crispy.
7. While the taquitos are baking, prepare the Avocado Ranch Dipping Sauce. Combine avocado, Greek yoghurt, mayonnaise, ranch seasoning mix, lime juice, salt, and pepper in a blender or food processor. Blend until smooth and creamy. Adjust seasoning to taste.
8. Once the taquitos are done, remove them from the oven and let them cool for a few minutes.
9. For dipping, serve the BBQ Chicken Taquitos warm with the Avocado Ranch Dipping Sauce on the side.

Nutrition: (NUTRITIONAL VALUES ARE APPROXIMATE AND WILL VARY DEPENDING ON SPECIFIC INGREDIENTS.)

- Calories: 380
- Total Fat: 18g
  - Saturated Fat: 5g
  - Trans Fat: 0g
- Cholesterol: 75mg
- Sodium: 810mg
- Total Carbohydrates: 29g
  - Dietary Fiber: 3g
  - Sugars: 12g

- Protein: 25g

SMOKED MOZZARELLA STICKS WITH MARINARA SAUCE

Cooking Time: 30 minutes
Servings: 4
Ingredients:

- 12 sticks of smoked mozzarella cheese, cut into 3-inch lengths
- 1 cup all-purpose flour
- Two large eggs, beaten
- 1 cup breadcrumbs
- One teaspoon Italian seasoning
- 1/2 teaspoon garlic powder
- 1/2 teaspoon onion powder
- Salt and pepper to taste
- Vegetable oil for frying

For the Marinara Sauce:

- One can (14 oz) crushed tomatoes
- Two cloves garlic, minced
- One tablespoon olive oil
- One teaspoon dried basil
- One teaspoon dried oregano
- Salt and pepper to taste

Directions:

1. **Prepare the Marinara Sauce:** Heat olive oil over medium heat in a saucepan. Add minced garlic and sauté until fragrant, about 1 minute. Stir in crushed tomatoes, basil, oregano, salt, and pepper. Bring to a simmer and cook for 10-15 minutes, stirring occasionally. Set aside.

2. **Prepare the Mozzarella Sticks:** Set up a breading station with three shallow bowls. Place flour in the first bowl, beaten eggs in the second bowl, and breadcrumbs mixed with Italian seasoning, garlic powder, onion powder, salt, and pepper in the third bowl.

3. Take each piece of smoked mozzarella and coat it in flour. Then, dip it into the beaten eggs and coat it thoroughly with the breadcrumb mixture. Set aside on a plate and repeat with the remaining cheese sticks.

4. Heat vegetable oil in a deep fryer or large skillet to 350°F (175°C).

5. Carefully place the coated mozzarella sticks into the hot oil in batches if necessary to avoid overcrowding. Fry for 2-3 minutes or until golden brown and crispy. Remove from the oil and drain on paper towels.

6. Serve the smoked mozzarella sticks immediately with the marinara sauce for dipping.

Nutrition:

- NUTRITIONAL INFORMATION IS APPROXIMATE AND MAY VARY DEPENDING ON INGREDIENTS AND PORTION SIZES.

- Calories per serving: Approximately 350 kcal

- Fat: 18g

- Carbohydrates: 30g

- Protein: 15g

- Fiber: 2g

GRILLED PIMENTO CHEESE STUFFED JALAPENOS

Cooking Time: 20 minutes
Servings: 6
Ingredients:

- 12 large jalapeno peppers

- 1 cup pimento cheese spread

- 1/4 cup shredded cheddar cheese

- One tablespoon chopped fresh cilantro (optional)

- Olive oil for brushing

Directions:

1. Preheat your grill to medium-high heat.

2. Slice each jalapeno pepper in half lengthwise and remove the seeds and membranes using a spoon. Wear gloves to protect your hands from the jalapeno oils.

3. Combine the pimento cheese spread, shredded cheddar cheese, and chopped cilantro, if desired, in a mixing bowl. Mix until well combined.

4. Spoon the pimento cheese mixture into each jalapeno half, filling them evenly.

5. Brush the stuffed jalapenos lightly with olive oil to prevent sticking on the grill.

6. Place the stuffed jalapenos on the preheated grill, cheese side up. Close the lid and grill for about 10-12 minutes, or until the peppers are tender and the cheese is melted and slightly browned.

7. Once done, carefully remove the grilled jalapenos from the grill using tongs.

8. Serve hot as a delicious appetizer or snack.

Nutrition:

- Calories: 180 kcal
- Protein: 8g
- Fat: 14g
- Carbohydrates: 5g
- Fiber: 1g
- Sugar: 2g
- Sodium: 320mg

TRAEGER SMOKED PRETZEL BITES WITH CHEESE DIP

Cooking Time: 2 hours

Servings: 6-8

Ingredients:

For the Pretzel Bites:

- 1 ½ cups warm water (110°F to 115°F)
- One packet (2 ¼ teaspoons) active dry yeast
- One tablespoon granulated sugar
- 4 cups all-purpose flour
- One teaspoon salt
- One egg, beaten (for egg wash)
- Coarse sea salt for sprinkling

For the Cheese Dip:

- 2 cups shredded cheddar cheese
- 1 cup shredded mozzarella cheese
- 1 cup milk
- Two tablespoons all-purpose flour
- Two tablespoons unsalted butter
- One teaspoon garlic powder
- Salt and pepper to taste

Directions:

1. **Prepare the Pretzel Dough:**
   - Combine warm water, yeast, and sugar in a large mixing bowl. Let it sit for 5-10 minutes until foamy.
   - Add flour and salt to the yeast mixture. Mix until a dough forms.
   - Knead the dough on a floured surface for about 5 minutes until smooth and elastic.

- Place the dough in a greased bowl, cover it with a clean kitchen towel, and let it rise in a warm place for about 1 hour or until doubled in size.

1. **Smoke the Pretzel Bites:**
   - Preheat your Traeger grill to 375°F according to manufacturer instructions.
   - Divide the dough into small pieces and roll each piece into a ball.
   - Bring water to a boil in a large pot and add baking soda.
   - Boil the pretzel bites in batches for about 30 seconds, then remove them with a slotted spoon and place them on a greased baking sheet.
   - Brush the pretzel bites with beaten egg and sprinkle them with coarse sea salt.
   - Place the baking sheet on the preheated Traeger grill and smoke for about 20-25 minutes until golden brown and cooked through.

1. **Prepare the Cheese Dip:**
   - In a saucepan, melt butter over medium heat. Add flour and cook, constantly stirring, for 1-2 minutes to make a roux.
   - Gradually whisk in milk until smooth and thickened.
   - Stir in shredded cheddar and mozzarella cheese until melted and creamy.
   - Add garlic powder, salt, and pepper to taste. Keep warm until ready to serve.

1. **Serve:**
   - Arrange the smoked pretzel bites alongside the warm cheese dip on a serving platter.
   - Enjoy your delicious Traeger smoked pretzel bites with cheese dip!

Nutrition (per serving): NUTRITIONAL VALUES MAY VARY DEPENDING ON PORTION SIZE AND INGREDIENTS USED.

- Calories: 350
- Fat: 15g
- Saturated Fat: 9g
- Cholesterol: 70mg
- Sodium: 750mg
- Carbohydrates: 40g
- Fiber: 2g
- Sugar: 2g
- Protein: 15g

SMOKED BBQ MEATBALLS WITH BOURBON GLAZE

Cooking Time: 1 hour 30 minutes
 Servings: 4-6
Ingredients:
For the meatballs:

- 1 pound ground beef

- 1/2 cup breadcrumbs

- 1/4 cup grated Parmesan cheese

- 1/4 cup finely chopped onion

- One large egg

- Two cloves garlic, minced

- One teaspoon dried oregano

- One teaspoon smoked paprika

- Salt and pepper to taste

For the bourbon glaze:

- 1 cup ketchup

- 1/4 cup bourbon

- Two tablespoons brown sugar

- Two tablespoons apple cider vinegar

- One tablespoon Worcestershire sauce

- One teaspoon Dijon mustard

- Salt and pepper to taste

Directions:

1. Preheat your smoker to 225°F (110°C).

2. In a large bowl, combine all the ingredients for the meatballs. Mix until everything is well combined.

3. Shape the mixture into 1-inch meatballs and place them on a smoker rack.

4. Smoke the meatballs for 1 hour or until they are cooked and have absorbed some smoky flavour.

5. While the meatballs are smoking, prepare the bourbon glaze. In a small saucepan, combine all the ingredients for the glaze over medium heat. Bring the mixture to a simmer and cook for about 10 minutes, stirring occasionally, until the glaze has thickened slightly.

6. Once the meatballs are cooked, remove them from the smoker and transfer them to a large bowl.

7. Pour the bourbon glaze over the meatballs and toss gently to coat them evenly.

8. Serve the smoked BBQ meatballs with bourbon glaze hot as an appetizer or a main dish with your favourite sides.

Nutrition:

- Calories: 350
- Fat: 15g
- Carbohydrates: 25g
- Protein: 25g
- Fiber: 1g
- Sugar: 13g

TRAEGER GRILLED BACON-WRAPPED SCALLOPS

Cooking Time: 20 minutes
Servings: 4
Ingredients:

- 16 large sea scallops
- Eight slices of bacon, cut in half
- Two tablespoons olive oil

- One teaspoon smoked paprika
- One teaspoon garlic powder
- Salt and pepper to taste
- Wooden skewers, soaked in water for 30 minutes

Directions:

1. Preheat your Traeger grill to 400°F (200°C) according to the manufacturer's instructions.
2. Rinse the scallops under cold water and pat them dry with paper towels. Season each scallop with smoked paprika, garlic powder, salt, and pepper.
3. Wrap each seasoned scallop with a half slice of bacon and secure it with a wooden skewer.
4. Brush each bacon-wrapped scallop with olive oil to prevent sticking.
5. Place the skewered scallops directly onto the preheated grill grates.
6. Grill the scallops for 10 minutes, then carefully flip them using tongs.
7. Continue grilling for another 8-10 minutes until the bacon is crispy and the scallops are cooked through. Be cautious not to overcook the scallops, as they can become rubbery.
8. Once done, remove the skewers from the grill and let the scallops rest for a few minutes before serving.

Nutrition: NOTE: NUTRITIONAL VALUES ARE APPROXIMATE AND MAY VARY DEPENDING ON SPECIFIC INGREDIENTS.

- Calories: 280 kcal
- Protein: 18g
- Fat: 21g
- Carbohydrates: 2g
- Fibre: 0g
- Sugars: 0g
- Sodium: 520mg

WOOD-FIRED BUFFALO CHICKEN DIP STUFFED PEPPERS

Cooking Time: 45 minutes

Servings: 6

Ingredients:

- Six large bell peppers (any colour), halved and seeds removed
- 2 cups cooked shredded chicken
- 1 cup cream cheese, softened
- 1/2 cup buffalo sauce
- 1/2 cup shredded mozzarella cheese
- 1/4 cup blue cheese crumbles
- 1/4 cup chopped green onions
- Salt and pepper to taste
- Optional garnish: chopped fresh parsley or additional green onions

Directions:

1. **Prepare the Grill:** Preheat your wood-fired grill to medium heat (about 375°F to 400°F).
2. **Prepare the Peppers:** Place the halved bell peppers on a baking sheet lined with aluminium foil and cut side up.
3. **Make the Filling:** In a large mixing bowl, combine the shredded chicken, softened cream cheese, buffalo sauce, shredded mozzarella cheese, blue cheese crumbles, chopped green onions, salt, and pepper. Mix until well combined.
4. **Stuff the Peppers:** Spoon the buffalo chicken dip mixture evenly into each bell pepper half, pressing down gently to fill them.
5. **Grill the Stuffed Peppers:** Carefully transfer the stuffed peppers to the preheated wood-fired grill. Close the lid and cook for about 25-30 minutes until the peppers are tender and the filling is heated through and bubbly.
6. **Serve:** Once cooked, remove the stuffed peppers from the grill and transfer them to a serving platter. Garnish with chopped fresh parsley or additional green onions if desired. Serve warm and enjoy!

Nutrition: (NUTRITIONAL VALUES ARE APPROXIMATE AND MAY VARY DEPENDING ON THE INGREDIENTS USED.)

- Calories: 280 kcal
- Total Fat: 18g
- Saturated Fat: 10g
- Cholesterol: 85mg
- Sodium: 650mg
- Total Carbohydrates: 10g

- Dietary Fiber: 2g
- Sugars: 5g
- Protein: 20g

GRILLED TERIYAKI BEEF SKEWERS WITH SESAME SEEDS

Cooking Time: 30 minutes
Servings: 4
Ingredients:

- 1 lb (450g) beef sirloin, cut into 1-inch cubes
- 1/2 cup teriyaki sauce
- Two tablespoons honey
- Two cloves garlic, minced
- One tablespoon fresh ginger, grated
- One tablespoon sesame oil
- One tablespoon sesame seeds
- Salt and pepper to taste
- Wooden skewers, soaked in water for 30 minutes

Directions:

1. Whisk together teriyaki sauce, honey, minced garlic, grated ginger, sesame oil, sesame seeds, salt, and pepper in a bowl.
2. Add the cubed beef to the marinade, ensuring all pieces are coated evenly. Cover and refrigerate for at least 1 hour or overnight for the best flavour.
3. Preheat your grill to medium-high heat.
4. Thread the marinated beef cubes onto the soaked wooden skewers, leaving a little space between each piece.
5. Place the skewers on the preheated grill and cook for about 3-4 minutes per side until the beef is cooked to your desired doneness and has nice grill marks.
6. While grilling, occasionally brush the skewers with the remaining marinade for extra flavour.
7. Once cooked, remove the skewers from the grill and let them rest for a few minutes.
8. Sprinkle with additional sesame seeds if desired before serving.

Nutrition (per serving):

- Calories: 290
- Total Fat: 15g
    - Saturated Fat: 5g
    - Trans Fat: 0g

- Cholesterol: 70mg
- Sodium: 960mg
- Total Carbohydrate: 12g
  - Dietary Fiber: 0.5g
  - Sugars: 9g
- Protein: 25g

SMOKED PROSCIUTTO-WRAPPED ASPARAGUS BUNDLES

Cooking Time: 20 minutes
Servings: 4
Ingredients:

- One bunch of asparagus, woody ends trimmed
- 8 slices of prosciutto
- Two tablespoons olive oil
- Salt and pepper to taste
- Optional: balsamic glaze for drizzling

Directions:

1. Preheat your grill or grill pan to medium-high heat.
2. Divide the asparagus spears into eight equal bundles, about 4-5 spears per bundle.
3. Take a slice of prosciutto and wrap it around each bundle of asparagus, ensuring the entire bundle is covered. You can wrap the prosciutto around the asparagus in a spiral pattern for a decorative touch.
4. Brush the wrapped asparagus bundles with olive oil and season with salt and pepper.
5. Place the bundles on the preheated grill or grill pan and cook for about 5-7 minutes, turning occasionally, until the asparagus is tender and the prosciutto is crispy.
6. Once cooked, transfer the bundles to a serving platter.
7. Optionally, drizzle with balsamic glaze for an extra burst of flavour.
8. Serve immediately and enjoy!

Nutrition: (per serving)

- Calories: 150 kcal
- Protein: 8g
- Fat: 10g
- Carbohydrates: 4g
- Fiber: 2g
- Sugar: 2g

- Sodium: 600mg

BBQ CHICKEN FLATBREAD WITH CARAMELIZED ONIONS

Cooking Time: 25 minutes

Servings: 4

Ingredients:

- Two pre-made flatbreads
- 2 cups cooked chicken, shredded or diced
- 1 cup BBQ sauce
- Two medium onions, thinly sliced
- Two tablespoons olive oil
- Salt and pepper to taste
- 1 cup shredded mozzarella cheese
- 1/4 cup chopped fresh cilantro (optional, for garnish)

Directions:

1. Preheat your oven to 400°F (200°C).
2. In a skillet, heat olive oil over medium heat. Add sliced onions and cook, stirring occasionally, until they are caramelized and golden brown, about 15-20 minutes. Season with salt and pepper to taste. Set aside.
3. In a mixing bowl, toss the cooked chicken with BBQ sauce until evenly coated.
4. Place the pre-made flatbreads on a baking sheet lined with parchment paper or sprayed with non-stick spray.
5. Spread the BBQ chicken mixture evenly over the flatbreads.
6. Top the BBQ chicken with the caramelized onions, distributing them evenly.
7. Sprinkle shredded mozzarella cheese over the top of each flatbread.
8. Bake in the preheated oven for about 10-12 minutes, or until the cheese is melted and bubbly and the edges of the flatbreads are crispy.
9. Once done, remove from the oven and let them cool slightly before slicing.
10. Garnish with chopped fresh cilantro, if desired.
11. Serve warm and enjoy!

Nutrition:

- NOTE: NUTRITION VALUES ARE APPROXIMATE AND MAY VARY DEPENDING ON SPECIFIC INGREDIENTS.
- Calories: 380 kcal
- Total Fat: 15g

- Saturated Fat: 5g

- Cholesterol: 65mg

- Sodium: 940mg

- Total Carbohydrates: 37g

- Dietary Fiber: 2g

- Sugars: 18g

- Protein: 23g

TRAEGER GRILLED STUFFED MUSHROOMS WITH CREAM CHEESE

Cooking Time: 30 minutes
Servings: 4
Ingredients:

- 12 large mushrooms, stems removed and reserved

- 8 ounces cream cheese, softened

- 1/4 cup grated Parmesan cheese

- Two cloves garlic, minced

- 1/4 cup chopped fresh parsley

- Salt and pepper to taste

- Olive oil for drizzling

- Optional: breadcrumbs for topping

Directions:

1. Preheat your Traeger grill to 375°F (190°C) according to manufacturer instructions.

2. Clean the mushrooms by gently wiping them with a damp paper towel. Remove the stems and chop them finely.

3. Combine the chopped mushroom stems, cream cheese, Parmesan cheese, minced garlic, chopped parsley, salt, and pepper in a mixing bowl. Mix until well combined.

4. Spoon the cream cheese mixture into each mushroom cap, filling them generously.

5. If desired, sprinkle breadcrumbs over the filled mushrooms for a crispy topping.

6. Drizzle olive oil over the stuffed mushrooms to help them cook and prevent sticking.

7. Place the stuffed mushrooms directly on the grill grates or use a grilling tray for easier handling.

8. Grill the mushrooms for 20-25 minutes or until the filling is hot and bubbly and the mushrooms are tender.

9. Once cooked, remove the stuffed mushrooms from the grill and serve hot.

Nutrition: NOTE: NUTRITIONAL VALUES MAY VARY DEPENDING ON THE INGREDIENTS USED.

- Calories: 220 kcal
- Total Fat: 18g
  - Saturated Fat: 10g
  - Trans Fat: 0g
- Cholesterol: 50mg
- Sodium: 350mg
- Total Carbohydrates: 6g
  - Dietary Fiber: 1g
  - Sugars: 2g
- Protein: 8g

WOOD-FIRED BRUSCHETTA WITH BALSAMIC GLAZE

Cooking Time: 15 minutes
Servings: 4
Ingredients:

- Four large ripe tomatoes, diced
- 1/4 cup fresh basil leaves, chopped
- Two cloves garlic, minced
- Two tablespoons extra virgin olive oil
- Salt and black pepper to taste
- 1 French baguette, sliced
- 1/4 cup balsamic glaze
- Fresh mozzarella cheese, sliced (optional)

Directions:

1. Preheat your wood-fired oven to about 400°F (200°C).

2. Combine diced tomatoes, chopped basil, minced garlic, extra virgin olive oil, salt, and black pepper in a mixing bowl. Toss gently to combine. Set aside to marinate while you prepare the bread.

3. Arrange the baguette slices on a baking sheet and lightly brush them with olive oil. Place them in the wood-fired oven until they are toasted and slightly crispy, about 5-7 minutes. Remove from the oven and set aside.

4. While the bread is still warm, spoon the tomato mixture generously over each slice.

5. Add a slice of fresh mozzarella on top of each bruschetta.

6. Return the topped bread to the wood-fired oven and bake for 5-7 minutes or until the cheese is melted and bubbly.

7. Once done, drizzle each bruschetta with balsamic glaze.

8. Serve immediately and enjoy the delicious wood-fired flavour!

Nutrition (per serving):

- Calories: 280 kcal
- Protein: 7g
- Fat: 10g
- Carbohydrates: 40g
- Fiber: 3g
- Sugar: 6g
- Sodium: 390mg

SMOKED BBQ CHICKEN NACHOS WITH HOMEMADE GUACAMOLE

Cooking Time: 40 minutes
Servings: 4-6
Ingredients:
For the BBQ Chicken:

- Two boneless, skinless chicken breasts
- 1 cup barbecue sauce
- One tablespoon olive oil
- Salt and pepper to taste

For the Nachos:

- One bag tortilla chips
- 1 cup shredded cheddar cheese
- 1 cup shredded Monterey Jack cheese
- 1/2 cup diced red onion

- 1/4 cup chopped fresh cilantro
- 1/4 cup sliced jalapeños (optional)
- 1/4 cup diced tomatoes
- 1/4 cup black beans (optional)
- 1/4 cup corn kernels (optional)

For the Homemade Guacamole:

- Two ripe avocados
- 1/4 cup diced red onion
- 1/4 cup diced tomato
- Two tablespoons chopped fresh cilantro
- One tablespoon lime juice
- Salt and pepper to taste

Directions:

1. **Prepare the BBQ Chicken:**
   - Preheat your smoker to 225°F (110°C).
   - Season the chicken breasts with salt and pepper.
   - Place the chicken breasts on the smoker and cook for 2-3 hours until the internal temperature reaches 165°F (75°C).
   - Once cooked, shred the chicken using two forks and toss it in barbecue sauce. Set aside.

1. **Make the Homemade Guacamole:**
   - Cut the avocados in half and remove the pits. Scoop out the flesh into a bowl.
   - Mash the avocado with a fork until desired consistency.
   - Stir in the diced red onion, diced tomato, chopped cilantro, lime juice, salt, and pepper. Adjust seasoning to taste.

1. **Assemble the Nachos:**
   - Preheat the oven to 350°F (175°C).
   - On a large baking sheet, spread out a layer of tortilla chips.
   - Sprinkle half of the shredded cheddar and Monterey Jack cheese over the chips.
   - Add the shredded BBQ chicken on top of the cheese layer.
   - Scatter diced red onion, chopped cilantro, jalapeños, tomatoes, black beans, and corn kernels over the chicken.
   - Top with the remaining shredded cheese.
   - Bake in the oven for 10-15 minutes or until the cheese is melted and bubbly.

1. **Serve:**
   - Remove the nachos from the oven and let them cool slightly.
   - Serve the nachos hot, accompanied by the homemade guacamole on the side.
   - Enjoy your delicious Smoked BBQ Chicken Nachos!

Nutrition: NOTE: NUTRITION VALUES MAY VARY DEPENDING ON THE INGREDIENTS USED.

- Calories: Approximately 400 per serving
- Total Fat: 25g
- Saturated Fat: 8g
- Cholesterol: 60mg
- Sodium: 600mg
- Total Carbohydrates: 30g
- Dietary Fiber: 5g
- Sugars: 8g
- Protein: 20g

GRILLED HONEY SRIRACHA CHICKEN WINGS

Cooking Time: 30 minutes
Servings: 4
Ingredients:

- 2 lbs chicken wings, split at joints and tips discarded
- 1/4 cup honey
- Three tablespoons Sriracha sauce
- Two tablespoons soy sauce
- Two cloves garlic, minced
- One tablespoon olive oil
- Salt and pepper to taste
- Sesame seeds and chopped green onions for garnish (optional)

Directions:

1. Whisk together honey, Sriracha sauce, soy sauce, minced garlic, olive oil, salt, and pepper in a large bowl.

2. Add chicken wings to the bowl and toss until they are evenly coated with the marinade. Let marinate in the refrigerator for at least 15 minutes or up to 1 hour.

3. Preheat the grill to medium-high heat.

4. Remove wings from the marinade and shake off excess. Reserve the marinade for basting.

5. Place wings on the grill and cook for about 20-25 minutes, turning occasionally, until cooked through and charred outside.

6. While grilling, occasionally baste the wings with the reserved marinade to keep them moist and flavorful.

7. Once cooked, remove the wings from the grill and place them on a serving platter.

8. Garnish with sesame seeds and chopped green onions if desired.

9. Serve hot and enjoy!

Nutrition:

- Calories: 320 kcal
- Protein: 24g
- Fat: 20g
- Carbohydrates: 12g
- Fiber: 0.5g
- Sugar: 11g
- Sodium: 720mg

BBQ PORK BELLY BURNT ENDS

Cooking Time: 4 hours

Servings: 6-8

Ingredients:

- 3 lbs pork belly, skin removed, cut into 1-inch cubes
- 1/4 cup BBQ rub seasoning
- 1/2 cup BBQ sauce
- 1/4 cup honey
- Two tablespoons brown sugar
- Two tablespoons butter
- Salt and black pepper to taste
- Wooden skewers, soaked in water (optional)

Directions:

1. **Preheat the Smoker:** Preheat your smoker to 250°F (120°C). For added flavour, wood chips or chunks for smoking, such as hickory, apple, or cherry.

2. **Prepare the Pork Belly:** Place the pork belly cubes in a large bowl. Season generously with BBQ rub seasoning, ensuring all pieces are evenly coated. Let it sit for about 15 minutes to allow the flavours to meld.

3. **Smoke the Pork Belly:** If using wooden skewers, thread several pieces of pork belly onto each skewer. This will make handling easier for the smoker. Otherwise, you can place the cubes directly on the smoker grate. Place the pork belly in the smoker and let it cook for 2-3 hours, or until the cubes develop a nice bark on the outside and are tender on the inside.

4. **Prepare the Glaze:** While the pork belly is smoking, prepare the glaze. Combine BBQ sauce, honey, brown sugar, and butter in a saucepan over medium heat. Stir until the

mixture is well combined and the sugar has dissolved. Let it simmer for about 5 minutes, then remove from heat.

5. **Finish the Burnt Ends:** Once the pork belly cubes have developed a good bark, remove them from the smoker and place them in a disposable aluminium pan. Pour the prepared glaze over the cubes, ensuring they are evenly coated.

6. **Return to the Smoker:** Return the pan of glazed pork belly to the smoker. Let it cook for 1-2 hours, or until the cubes are caramelized and tender, stirring occasionally to ensure even coating with the glaze.

7. **Serve:** Once done, remove the BBQ pork belly burnt ends from the smoker and let them rest for a few minutes. Serve hot as a delicious appetizer or a main dish with your favourite sides.

Nutrition: NOTE: NUTRITION INFORMATION MAY VARY DEPENDING ON THE INGREDIENTS AND QUANTITIES USED.

- Calories: 450 kcal
- Protein: 20g
- Fat: 35g
- Carbohydrates: 12g
- Fiber: 1g
- Sugar: 10g
- Sodium: 650mg

TRAEGER SMOKED SHRIMP COCKTAIL WITH SPICY COCKTAIL SAUCE

Cooking Time: 30 minutes
Servings: 4
Ingredients:
For the Smoked Shrimp:

- 1 pound large shrimp, peeled and deveined
- Two tablespoons olive oil
- Two teaspoons smoked paprika
- One teaspoon garlic powder
- Salt and pepper to taste

For the Spicy Cocktail Sauce:

- 1 cup ketchup
- Two tablespoons prepared horseradish
- One tablespoon lemon juice
- One teaspoon Worcestershire sauce

- One teaspoon hot sauce (adjust to taste)
- Salt and pepper to taste

For Serving:

- Lemon wedges
- Fresh parsley, chopped (optional)
- Iceberg lettuce leaves (optional)

Directions:

1. **Prepare the Smoker:** Preheat your Traeger smoker to 225°F (107°C) according to the manufacturer's instructions.

2. **Prepare the Shrimp:** In a large bowl, toss the shrimp with olive oil, smoked paprika, garlic powder, salt, and pepper until evenly coated.

3. **Smoke the Shrimp:** Place the seasoned shrimp directly on the grill grates of the smoker. Close the lid and smoke for about 20-25 minutes, or until the shrimp are pink and opaque, flipping them halfway through the cooking time.

4. **Prepare the Spicy Cocktail Sauce:** In a small bowl, combine ketchup, horseradish, lemon juice, Worcestershire sauce, hot sauce, salt, and pepper. Mix well to combine. Adjust the seasoning according to your taste preferences.

5. **Serve:** Arrange the smoked shrimp on a platter with iceberg lettuce leaves if desired. Serve with the spicy cocktail sauce on the side. Garnish with lemon wedges and chopped parsley, if desired.

Nutrition:

NOTE: NUTRITIONAL VALUES ARE APPROXIMATE AND MAY VARY DEPENDING ON SPECIFIC INGREDIENTS.

- Calories: 250 kcal
- Protein: 25g
- Fat: 8g
- Carbohydrates: 20g
- Fiber: 2g
- Sugar: 15g
- Sodium: 1100mg

WOOD-FIRED SPINACH AND FETA STUFFED MINI PEPPERS

Cooking Time: 25 minutes
Servings: 4
Ingredients:

- 12 mini sweet peppers
- 1 cup fresh spinach, chopped

- 1/2 cup crumbled feta cheese
- 1/4 cup grated Parmesan cheese
- Two cloves garlic, minced
- One tablespoon olive oil
- Salt and pepper to taste
- Fresh basil leaves for garnish (optional)

Directions:

1. Preheat your wood-fired oven to 400°F (200°C). If using a regular oven, preheat to the same temperature.
2. Wash the mini sweet peppers, cut off the tops and remove the seeds and membranes. Set aside.
3. In a skillet, heat olive oil over medium heat. Add minced garlic and sauté for 1-2 minutes until fragrant.
4. Add chopped spinach to the skillet and cook until wilted, about 2-3 minutes. Season with salt and pepper to taste.
5. Remove the skillet from heat and transfer the cooked spinach to a mixing bowl. Let it cool slightly.
6. Once cooled, add crumbled feta cheese and grated Parmesan cheese to the bowl with spinach. Mix well to combine.
7. Stuff each mini sweet pepper with the spinach and feta mixture, pressing gently to fill them evenly.
8. Place stuffed peppers on a baking sheet or in a cast-iron skillet and transfer to the preheated wood-fired oven.
9. Bake for 10-12 minutes until the peppers are tender, and the filling is heated through and slightly golden on top.
10. Once done, remove it from the oven and let it cool for a few minutes before serving.
11. Garnish with fresh basil leaves if desired, and serve warm.

Nutrition:

- **Calories:** 120 kcal
- **Protein:** 5g
- **Fat:** 8g
- **Carbohydrates:** 8g
- **Fiber:** 2g
- **Sodium:** 280mg

GRILLED CAPRESE SKEWERS WITH BALSAMIC REDUCTION

Cooking Time: 15 minutes
Servings: 4
Ingredients:

- 1 pint cherry tomatoes

- 8 ounces fresh mozzarella cheese, cut into cubes

- Fresh basil leaves

- Two tablespoons olive oil

- Salt and pepper to taste

- Balsamic reduction (store-bought or homemade)

Directions:

1. Preheat your grill to medium-high heat.

2. Thread the cherry tomatoes, mozzarella cubes, and fresh basil leaves onto skewers, alternating between the ingredients.

3. Brush the assembled skewers with olive oil and sprinkle with salt and pepper.

4. Place the skewers on the preheated grill and cook for 2-3 minutes per side until the tomatoes are slightly charred and the cheese softens.

5. Once grilled, transfer the skewers to a serving platter.

6. Drizzle the balsamic reduction over the skewers just before serving.

7. Serve immediately and enjoy!

Nutrition (per serving):

- Calories: 220 kcal

- Protein: 12g

- Fat: 16g

- Carbohydrates: 9g

- Fiber: 2g

- Sugar: 5g

- Sodium: 280mg

SMOKED SALMON CROSTINI WITH HERBED CREAM CHEESE

Cooking Time: 15 minutes
Servings: 6-8
Ingredients:

- One baguette, thinly sliced

- 200g smoked salmon, thinly sliced

- 250g cream cheese, softened
- Two tablespoons fresh dill, chopped
- One tablespoon fresh chives, chopped
- One tablespoon fresh lemon juice
- Salt and black pepper to taste

Directions:

1. Preheat your oven to 375°F (190°C).
2. Place the baguette slices on a baking sheet and toast them in the oven for 5-7 minutes or until they are lightly golden and crisp. Remove them from the oven and let them cool slightly.
3. Combine the softened cream cheese, chopped dill, chives, and lemon juice in a mixing bowl. Mix well until smooth. Season with salt and black pepper according to your taste.
4. Spread a generous layer of the herbed cream cheese mixture onto each toasted baguette slice.
5. Top each crostini with a slice of smoked salmon.
6. Garnish with additional chopped dill or chives if desired.
7. Arrange the prepared crostini on a serving platter and serve immediately.

Nutrition:

- **Calories:** 220 kcal
- **Total Fat:** 12g
- **Saturated Fat:** 6g
- **Cholesterol:** 35mg
- **Sodium:** 450mg
- **Total Carbohydrates:** 18g
- **Dietary Fiber:** 1g
- **Sugars:** 2g
- **Protein:** 10g

BBQ PULLED CHICKEN SLIDERS WITH COLESLAW

Cooking Time: 4 hours
Servings: 6
Ingredients:

- 2 lbs boneless, skinless chicken breasts
- 1 cup BBQ sauce
- 1/4 cup brown sugar

- One tablespoon Worcestershire sauce
- One teaspoon smoked paprika
- 1/2 teaspoon garlic powder
- 1/2 teaspoon onion powder
- Salt and pepper to taste
- 12 slider buns
- For the coleslaw:
  - 3 cups shredded cabbage
  - One carrot, grated
  - 1/2 cup mayonnaise
  - Two tablespoons apple cider vinegar
  - One tablespoon honey
  - Salt and pepper to taste

Directions:

1. Combine BBQ sauce, brown sugar, Worcestershire sauce, smoked paprika, garlic powder, onion powder, salt, and pepper in a slow cooker. Mix well.
2. Add the chicken breasts to the slow cooker, coating them with the BBQ sauce.
3. Cook on low for 4 hours or until the chicken is tender and easily shreds with a fork.
4. While the chicken is cooking, prepare the coleslaw. In a large bowl, combine shredded cabbage and grated carrots.
5. Whisk together mayonnaise, apple cider vinegar, honey, salt, and pepper in a separate small bowl to make the dressing.
6. Pour the dressing over the cabbage and carrot mixture. Toss until well coated. Refrigerate until ready to use.
7. Once the chicken is cooked, shred it using two forks directly in the slow cooker, mixing it well with the BBQ sauce.
8. Place a generous amount of pulled chicken onto the bottom half of each slider bun to assemble the sliders.
9. Top the pulled chicken with a spoonful of coleslaw.
10. Place the top half of the slider bun on top and secure with a toothpick if needed.
11. Serve immediately and enjoy!

Nutrition: (PER SERVING)
Calories: 450
Total Fat: 15g
Saturated Fat: 3g
Cholesterol: 95mg
Sodium: 850mg
Total Carbohydrate: 45g

Dietary Fiber: 3g
Sugars: 19g
Protein: 35g

TRAEGER GRILLED BACON-WRAPPED JALAPENO POPPERS

Cooking Time: 30 minutes
Servings: 10
Ingredients:

- Ten large jalapeno peppers
- One package (8 ounces) cream cheese, softened
- 1 cup shredded cheddar cheese
- Ten slices of bacon
- One teaspoon garlic powder
- One teaspoon onion powder
- One teaspoon smoked paprika
- Toothpicks

Directions:

1. Preheat your Traeger grill to 375°F (190°C) according to manufacturer instructions.
2. Cut the jalapenos in half lengthwise and remove the seeds and membranes. Use caution and gloves to avoid contact with the jalapeno oils.
3. Combine the softened cream cheese, shredded cheddar cheese, garlic powder, onion powder, and smoked paprika in a mixing bowl. Mix until well combined.
4. Fill each jalapeno half with the cheese mixture, ensuring they are evenly filled.
5. Wrap each stuffed jalapeno half with a slice of bacon, securing it with toothpicks to hold it in place.
6. Place the bacon-wrapped jalapeno poppers directly on the grill grate of your Traeger grill.
7. Grill the poppers for about 20-25 minutes, turning once halfway through the cooking time, until the bacon is crispy and the jalapenos are tender.
8. Once done, remove the jalapeno poppers from the grill and let them cool for a few minutes before serving.

Nutrition: (PER SERVING)

- Calories: 215
- Total Fat: 18g
    - Saturated Fat: 9g
    - Trans Fat: 0g
- Cholesterol: 49mg

- Sodium: 365mg
- Total Carbohydrates: 2g
  - Dietary Fiber: 0g
  - Sugars: 1g
- Protein: 10g

WOOD-FIRED GARLIC PARMESAN GRILLED SHRIMP

Cooking Time: 15 minutes
Servings: 4
Ingredients:

- 1 pound large shrimp, peeled and deveined
- Three cloves garlic, minced
- 1/4 cup grated Parmesan cheese
- Two tablespoons olive oil
- One tablespoon fresh lemon juice
- One teaspoon dried oregano
- Salt and pepper to taste
- Wooden skewers, soaked in water for 30 minutes

Directions:

1. Preheat your wood-fired grill to medium-high heat.
2. Combine minced garlic, Parmesan cheese, olive oil, lemon juice, dried oregano, salt, and pepper in a bowl. Mix well to create a marinade.
3. Add the peeled and deveined shrimp to the marinade. Toss until the shrimp are evenly coated. Let them marinate for 10 minutes.
4. Thread the marinated shrimp onto the soaked wooden skewers, leaving a little space between each shrimp.
5. Place the shrimp skewers on the preheated wood-fired grill. Cook for 2-3 minutes on each side until the shrimp are pink and opaque.
6. Once cooked, remove the shrimp skewers from the grill and transfer them to a serving platter.
7. Garnish with freshly chopped parsley and lemon wedges if desired.
8. Serve hot and enjoy your delicious wood-fired garlic Parmesan grilled shrimp!

Nutrition (per serving):

- Calories: 215 kcal
- Protein: 24g
- Fat: 11g

- Carbohydrates: 2g
- Fiber: 0.5g
- Sugar: 0.5g

SMOKED BBQ BEEF SLIDERS WITH PICKLES AND ONIONS

Cooking Time: 4 hours (including smoking time)
Servings: 6-8
Ingredients:

- 2 pounds of beef brisket
- 1 cup BBQ sauce
- One teaspoon smoked paprika
- One teaspoon garlic powder
- One teaspoon onion powder
- Salt and pepper to taste
- 12-16 slider buns
- Sliced pickles
- Sliced onions

Directions:

1. Preheat your smoker to 225°F (107°C).
2. Season the beef brisket generously with smoked paprika, garlic powder, onion powder, salt, and pepper.
3. Place the seasoned brisket in the smoker and smoke for 4 hours, or until the internal temperature reaches 195°F (90°C) and the meat is tender.
4. Remove the brisket from the smoker and let it rest for 15-20 minutes.
5. Using two forks, shred the smoked brisket.
6. In a large skillet, heat the BBQ sauce over medium heat. Add the shredded brisket to the skillet and toss until evenly coated with the sauce. Cook for an additional 5 minutes.
7. To assemble the sliders, place a generous amount of the BBQ beef on the bottom half of each slider bun.
8. Top with sliced pickles and onions.
9. Place the top half of the slider bun on top and secure with a toothpick.
10. Serve immediately and enjoy!

Nutrition:

- Serving Size: 1 slider
- Calories: 350

- Total Fat: 12g

- Saturated Fat: 4g

- Cholesterol: 80mg

- Sodium: 600mg

- Total Carbohydrates: 32g

- Dietary Fiber: 2g

- Sugars: 10g

- Protein: 26g

GRILLED TERIYAKI CHICKEN LETTUCE WRAPS

Cooking Time: 25 minutes
Servings: 4
Ingredients:

- 1 lb boneless, skinless chicken breasts cut into thin strips

- 1/2 cup teriyaki sauce

- Two tablespoons soy sauce

- Two cloves garlic, minced

- One tablespoon sesame oil

- One tablespoon honey

- One teaspoon grated fresh ginger

- 1/4 teaspoon red pepper flakes (optional)

- One tablespoon vegetable oil

- One head iceberg or butter lettuce, leaves separated

- 1/4 cup sliced green onions

- 1/4 cup chopped cilantro

- Sesame seeds for garnish (optional)

Directions:

1. Combine teriyaki sauce, soy sauce, minced garlic, sesame oil, honey, grated ginger, and red pepper flakes in a bowl. Mix well to combine.

2. Place the chicken strips in a shallow dish or resealable plastic bag. Pour half of the teriyaki marinade over the chicken, reserving the other half for later. Ensure the chicken is well coated, then cover and refrigerate for at least 15 minutes or up to 1 hour.

3. Preheat your grill to medium-high heat. Brush the grill grates with vegetable oil to prevent sticking.

4. Remove the chicken from the marinade, shaking off any excess. Discard the used marinade.

5. Grill the chicken strips for 3-4 minutes per side until cooked through and nicely charred on the edges. Ensure the chicken's internal temperature reaches 165°F (75°C).

6. While the chicken is grilling, heat the reserved teriyaki marinade in a small saucepan over medium heat. Bring it to a simmer and cook for 2-3 minutes until slightly thickening. Remove from heat.

7. Once the chicken is cooked, remove it from the grill and rest for a few minutes. Then, slice it into thin strips.

8. Place a spoonful of grilled chicken onto each lettuce leaf to assemble the lettuce wraps. Top with sliced green onions, chopped cilantro, and a drizzle of the warmed teriyaki sauce.

9. Sprinkle sesame seeds over the top for garnish, if desired.

10. Serve immediately and enjoy!

Nutrition (per serving):

- Calories: 250
- Total Fat: 8g
- Saturated Fat: 1.5g
- Cholesterol: 80mg
- Sodium: 1200mg
- Total Carbohydrates: 12g
- Dietary Fiber: 1g
- Sugars: 9g
- Protein: 30g

CONCLUSION

We hope that as you end your journey through the "Traeger Grill & Smoker Cookbook," you have gained a deeper appreciation for the art of barbecue. We believe that this guide's new ideas, techniques, and recipes will help you elevate your grilling game and become a true barbecue master. Thank you for choosing our cookbook, and we wish you happy grilling!

Whether planning a casual backyard cookout, hosting a tailgate party, or preparing for a private family event, we are confident that the professional advice, innovative methods, and mouthwatering recipes in this cookbook will help you create a memorable culinary experience that your guests will love.

As you continue to hone your skills and explore the endless possibilities of outdoor cooking, always remember that barbecuing is more than just about the food. While the delicious flavours and aromas are certainly a highlight, the true essence of grilling lies in spending quality time with your loved ones, making lasting memories, and appreciating the simple things in life.

So, whether you're a seasoned pitmaster or a novice grill enthusiast, we encourage you to connect with your inner chef, fire up your Traeger grill, and savour every moment of your barbecue journey. We hope your grill stays hot, your smoke remains sweet, and your barbecue remains amazing indefinitely. Thank you for joining us on this delightful voyage, and here's to many more enjoyable days ahead! Cheers!

Made in United States
Orlando, FL
01 May 2024

46386969R00076